NETWORK YOUR WAY TO SUCCESS*

*Ken Erdman and Tom Sullivan
Show You How

Marketers Bookshelf
Philadelphia, PA 19118

A Marketers Bookshelf Book / June, 1992

NETWORK YOUR WAY TO SUCCESS

Edited by: **Anne Dierkes**

Cover design and artwork: Sam Morley, Sun Design
Typesetting and page design: Anne Dierkes

For information:
Marketers Bookshelf
402 Bethlehem Pike
Philadelphia, PA 19118
(215) 247-2787
FAX: (215) 233-2203

ISBN Number 0-939951-02-9

Library of Congress Catalog Card Number 90-64271

Printed in the United States of America

DEDICATIONS

Dedicated to Murray Raphel, my good friend, business associate and mentor.

More than thirty years ago I read a direct mail column which Murray had written in the *Reporter of Direct Mail Advertising* (now *Direct Marketing Magazine*).

I was so impressed both by what he had to say and his writing style that I phoned him at his business in Atlantic City, New Jersey. I wanted to include Murray in my network of exciting people. Thus began a long friendship and business association.

Since then Murray Raphel and I have co-authored a book, traveled together to speak on the same platforms in various countries of the world, shared ideas for each other's clients and especially enjoyed a rewarding friendship.

All of this as a result of just one networking phone call!

Ken Erdman

This book is dedicated to Don Craighead for whom networking is a way of life. Had I not met Don you would not be reading this book.

Ken Erdman lives in Philadelphia and I live in Minneapolis. How do two people, over a thousand miles apart, decide to write a book together? Though we didn't know each other, Don knew each of us as writers and networkers. He suggested, "Why don't you two guys get together and write a book on networking?"

I have learned from Don about the power of networking in getting things done. He has taught me what giving is all about, and what "Service Above Self" (official motto of Rotary International) really means.

Thanks, Don, good friend, mentor and consummate networker.

Tom Sullivan

CONTENTS

Part Two: Casting Your Net
Developing Your Network

Part Three: Bringing In Your Catch
The Techniques of Networking

SUCCESS STORIES

"Are you devoting the bulk of your marketing effort, dollars, and energy to activating a word-of-mouth network? Are all your salespersons devoting a specific – and sizeable – share of time to user network development and expansion? Is every employee a conscientious network developer among his or her colleagues? If you answer 'no' to any of these questions, you may be turning your back on your highest-leverage market-development activity."

Tom Peters
author of
In Search Of Excellence

FOREWORD

The dictionary defines the word *network* as, "An interconnected or interrelated chain, group or system." A network is most commonly referred to when speaking of a radio or television network of stations. Corporations have their networks of hotels, restaurants, service stations, etc. All of these networks have one very important element in common, they all are run by *people*. And it is ultimately the networking and communication of people that is important.

A more practical definition of network could be, "The introduction of people with common interests to each other." Another description of networking could be, "word of mouth." More often than not it is through "word of mouth" or a network system that we sell and buy products, meet new acquaintances and find meaningful employment.

Network Your Way To Success is a book whose time has come. It shows you how, in detail, you can build your own network. It documents how people from varying backgrounds effectively use networking – in subtle and not so subtle ways – to help them achieve their individual successes. The examples shown will introduce you to new and innovative ways to network. They will remind you of some old networking techniques you forgot about and inspire you to be even more creative in thinking about how you can *network your way to success!*

Networking has been very important in my business life, helping me secure needed resources, both human and material, to achieve my dreams and goals. But more importantly, networking has demonstrated to me the value of the human being and introduced me to a multitude of new friends who have become my extended family.

The late Robert Muller, who had a way of getting to the core of the matter, wrote what I believe to be the ultimate piece on networking. It is titled, "Decide To Network."

Decide to network
Use every letter you write
Every conversation you have
Every meeting you attend
To express your fundamental beliefs and dreams
Affirm to others the vision of the world you want
Network through thought
Network through action
Network through love
Network through the spirit
You are the center of a network
You are the center of the world
You are a free, immensely powerful source
of life and goodness
Affirm it
Spread it
Radiate it
Think day and night about it
And you will see a miracle happen
the greatness of your own life
In a world of big powers, media and monopolies
Networking is the new freedom
the new democracy
a new form of happiness.

I truly believe, when all is said and done, networking is just another way of saying, "people helping people."

Aloha,

Wally "Famous" Amos
National Spokesperson for Literacy

INTRODUCTION

You are about to enter into a new and dynamic lifestyle.

As audacious as that may sound, the exciting personal stories in this book demonstrate that lives can indeed be richer and fuller as a direct result of having applied the principles of networking.

In our book, you'll learn how to turn casual relationships into an ever growing circle of personal friends. Expert help with almost any kind of problem will be at your fingertips. You'll spend much less time, money and effort to gain new customers, clients or patients. Your social life will expand. Personal success and happiness can be had through networking.

And yes, this book is about making money. Not necessarily making money "the old fashioned way," but making money as a result of the pursuit of wealth and the pursuit of happiness yoked together. Combined, these two can be one team to pull you through life with the satisfaction of being appreciated and the instant rewards of knowing you've helped someone else.

Networking is not for personal gain alone. Throughout our book we'll teach – nay preach – that to receive you'll have to give.

Networking isn't about the "good old boys" networks. It's about open minded people looking for like kind. It's not the age (as in good *old* boys) that counts, nor is it the boys (as in good old *boys*) that count. Our book is for any age and either sex.

It's attitude and discipline that count for networkers. You have to want to network your way to success and have the discipline to follow through and build your network.

We believe in networking. It has dramatically changed our lives. This book is a direct result of both of us applying the principles of networking.

Here's the story of our book...

Tom Sullivan wrote an earlier book, ***Network Your Net Worth***. Don Craighead, a Minnesota executive, was so impressed with the book and its concepts, he contacted Tom and thus a new friendship developed for both of them. Then Don wrote to Ken Erdman and complimented him on a magazine article Ken had written. Don suggested Ken network with his other writer friend, Tom.

Through Don we had discovered our mutual interest in networking. We then decided to meet, and from that short airport meeting, the two of us decided to collaborate on this book.

If you've bought this book, then networking has worked for us. If you read this book and apply its principals, networking will work for you. You really can ***Network Your Way To Success.***

Ken Erdman

Tom Sullivan

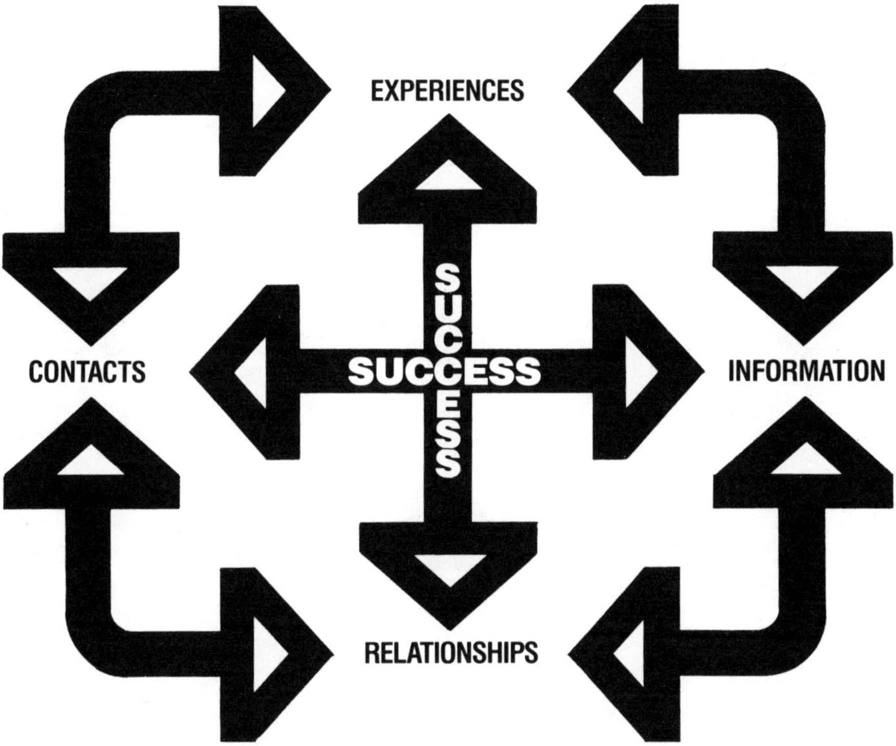

No matter where the networking process begins, it will be enhanced along the way by **contacts, relationships, experiences** and **information.** The integration of these concepts into your daily activities will become a positive force in your efforts to *network your way to success.*

Part One

Weaving Your Net

How Networking Works

1

What Is Networking?

And how you can tap its power

It's happening millions of times each day. In the work place, at home, at the club, in restaurants, supermarkets, churches. On planes, trains and boats; on the golf course, on street corners and even at the beach.

It's aided by business cards, the telephone, fax machines, voice mail, letters, advertisements, gifts and meetings.

It involves sales people, volunteers, singles, travelers, business people, professionals, employees, organization members, hobbyists, retired people and family members.

It helps people solve problems, find jobs, get promoted, acquire clients and patients, enlist volunteers, develop hobbies, improve their love lives, make more money *and become more successful.*

What is this pervasive communications phenomenon?

It's ***networking.***

NETWORKING: DEFINED AND REFINED

Almost everyone at one time or another has used some form of networking. Yet only in recent years has this system of extensive personal contacts been defined and refined.

Networking has been defined as a system used to develop contacts among business people. John Naisbitt, futurist and author of the 6-million-copy bestseller ***Megatrends***, describes networking as, "People talking to each other, sharing ideas, information and resources. Networks are structured to transmit information in a way that is quicker, more energy efficient, more high tech than any other process we know..." From Jessica Lipnack and Jeffrey Stamps, authors of ***The Networking Book***: "A network is a web of freestanding participants cohering through shared values and interests. Networking is people connecting with people, linking ideas and resources." Fred Smith, in his book ***You and Your Network***, refers to networking as "organized assistance."

In "The Art of Networking," an article in ***Success*** magazine, author Steve Fishman refers to a networker who describes networks as social clubs without premises.

In more technical language, behavioral scientists describe networks as "loosely organized systems" (or "LOS") – those communications systems where there are personal attachments.

We sum up all of these definitions into two words: *disciplined acquaintanceship*.

"Acquaintanceship" gives our definition broad coverage. Our version of networking is not just the traditional networking primarily used among business people or within the "old boys" school. Networking is not used exclusively for making money, although making money is often the by-product of effective networking. It is a process by which we make personal contacts to help us achieve success.

THE THREE P's OF NETWORKING

Our networking is a *Positive* process. It is about developing *Personal* relationships among the various levels of people with whom we're involved on a regular basis. These elements in combination produce a kind of *Power* networking which leads to increased success, both professionally and socially.

In a recent workshop on networking, Roni Dordick of Florida opened the program by indicating that she had networked for years but had never given a name to the process. She described her previous, somewhat unstructured method of calling on other people for information and help. Now, in an effort to further expand her resources, she uses *all* of the tools of networking at her disposal to organize and utilize her collection of acquaintances. She has transformed a casual habit into a structured, positive force to seek out the people who can be of personal help to her. Her networking has resulted not only in gaining her a new job but has also started her on the road to teaching workshops on the subject of networking.

BEYOND PERSONAL NETWORKS

In addition to networks composed of personal relationships, there are many other kinds of networks where people and organizations work together as units. A unit is a loose collection of identifiable groups with similar aims or goals or highly structured businesses under a common umbrella. Typically, you will find networks among employees in corporations (small teams and other decentralized units), networks among similar businesses and professions, information networks and networks of people with like interests. You'll recognize many of them by the name "network" in their titles. The 1991 New York City phone book lists 27 organizations whose names begin with "network." Commonly known business networks are the TV networks – CBS, NBC, ABC, etc. Many business and professional associations are really networks on a formal and structured basis. Although these group networks accomplish much the same goals as personal networks, they tend to be self-limiting to narrower interests – people interested in particular subjects or activities.

NETWORKING IN THE 90's

Networking, in one form or another, has been around almost since the beginning of time. It's only in recent years that the concept has been formally acknowledged.

With the advent of inexpensive yet sophisticated computers, fax machines, voice mail, mobile telephones, automatic telephone dialing, and a host of other electronic wizardry, new techniques have evolved to provide instant access to not only the names of the people in your networks, but to the people themselves.

In *Megatrends*, author John Naisbitt describes networking as one of the ten new directions transforming our lives. In his later book *Re-Inventing the Corporation*, Naisbitt suggests, "The top down authoritarian style is yielding to a networking style of management, where people learn from one another horizontally, where everyone is a resource for everyone else and where each person gets support and assistance from many different directions."

The words of author Tom Peters which are highlighted at the beginning of our book, are worth repeating and emphasizing:

> "Are you devoting the bulk of your marketing effort, dollars and energy to activating a word-of-mouth network? Are all of your salespeople devoting a specific – and sizeable – share of time to user network development and expansion? Is every employee a conscientious network developer among his or her colleagues? If you answer 'no' to any of these questions, you may be turning your back on your highest-leverage market-development activity."

In his book *Corporate Networking*, Robert K. Mueller says, "The concept of human networks and the process of social networking are prime components for a properly balanced organizational system in these turbulent and exciting times."

There are those that consider the concept of networking to be a fad of the 80's. We predict, however, that with the improved equipment which will enable networkers to better catalog and reach people, and the personal discipline of networkers to actively pursue these contacts, networking will continue to be a major communications strategy through the 90's. Networking just works too well to be relegated to a fad status.

NETWORKING VERSUS SCHMOOZING

In a 1990 ***Los Angeles Daily News*** column, writer Diana E. Lundin defines schmoozing as, "friendly, gossipy conversation, often with undertones of promoting an agenda," and suggests that schmoozing is a way to sweeten a sales pitch. (The word "schmooze" comes from the Yiddish, meaning to gossip or report, and describes the friendly, chatty way Jewish merchants conducted business.) Lundin calls Los Angeles, "the schmooze capital of the world."

Minneapolis Star Tribune writer Ellen Foley took umbrage with Lundin. In a rebuttal article she said, "Attention power schmoozers from Los Angeles. Be advised that in Minnesota we don't schmooze, we *network*." (It's no coincidence that co-author of this book, Tom Sullivan, hails from Minnesota.)

Schmoozing, as we see it, is strictly an in-person technique – to be used during the cocktail party, luncheon, golf date, trade show or convention. Networking, although it includes schmoozing as an important element, is far more comprehensive, embracing a wide variety of tools and techniques.

CAN I *REALLY* NETWORK MY WAY TO SUCCESS?

YES! Definitely!

The amount of success, however, depends on your personal goals and initiative. Do you want to get ahead in your job? Do you want to make more sales? Do you want to increase your circle of friends? Do you want to find a mate? Do you want to participate more fully in an organization? Do you need special information or help? Do you want to always be able to find just the right person to do a particular job? Are you willing to spend time developing and maintaining a list of contacts...and then spend time working that list?

Though they may not lay claim to the title, most successful people are good networkers. They have the same needs and desires that you have, and they are willing to regularly devote time to the networking process.

This book's promise is to show you how to network to achieve both business and social success. Taking advantage of a well organized database (a catalog of names and information), the planned use of business cards, the telephone, fax machine, direct mail, public relations efforts, greetings, memos, newsletters and other techniques, you can favorably increase your visibility, and access people who can help you become successful.

Not only will you learn how to use the tools of networking, but you will also read fascinating stories about highly successful people who have used these same tools to reach their goals and achieve business and personal success.

Best of all, networking need not be expensive in either money or time. Most of the tools are already available to you, and with a little organization you'll be surprised at how easily you'll find the necessary time to be a disciplined networker.

2

Building Your Personal Network

How many people do you really know?

Let's try a fun exercise. Consider how many people you know. Start with your personal telephone/address book. Next add in the names from your business phone/address system. Now you have the beginnings of your list.

Have you overlooked anybody? How about your church directory – the people there that you've known for years, but who don't appear in your own telephone or address book. And your country club membership roster. Your alumnae association from college (and high school). How about names of people you know well from the rosters of your trade or professional associations, charitable groups, civic and service clubs? Wow! What a list! And that's just the tip of the iceberg.

We still haven't added the names of the people with whom we come in contact on a daily basis whose names are not included in any of the sources we mentioned. There's Bill, the manager of our favorite restaurant. We've eaten there for years but Bill's name is not to be found on any of our lists. And the shoemaker. We usually don't have a frequent need to call him, so his name is not on our lists. Then there are new neighbors. How about old neighbors you've never had a chance to meet?

You might even meet potential networkers in the hot tub. Might? One of us did! While working (!) in Hawaii, Ken overheard a conversation between two exhibitors at a trade show being held across the street at the Hilton Hawaiian Village. Interested, Ken asked what show they were discussing. One of the salesmen replied, "It's a show for country club managers." "Well," Ken said, "I guess *my* club manager won't be here. I'm from way back on the East coast."

"What club do you belong to?" was the next question. "Manufacturers' Golf and Country Club," Ken replied. The exhibitor said, "Don Steckler, your manager, is here. I just saw him this morning!"

That chance bit of networking led to breakfast the next day with Don and Ken and their wives. And that breakfast led to a project for Ken with the country club.

Have you now noticed that you are part of a vast, rich, ever-expanding network? You're *not* starting from scratch. Now you have your own personal extensive "yellow pages." Within them, you can probably find every resource you'll ever need.

You really know more people than you thought you did. If you are reading this book burdened by the thought that you have to *find* a network, relax – all you have to do is learn to build on the one you're in right now.

Don't try to do it all at once. Like any good system, it pays to start out slowly. If you join the local Chamber of Commerce, two new associations, and a health club with the intention of really networking, it isn't going to work. Networking has to become a life style, and life styles are built slowly.

DISCIPLINED ACQUAINTANCESHIP

Some of these people we know better than others, but for all of them, there is at least an acquaintance relationship (remember our definition, *disciplined acquaintanceship*).

The first discipline of networking is to organize the names of these acquaintances and determine their importance to our network – to identify those who will be most helpful in a given situation.

Your databank (list of names along with pertinent information) can be divided into four main categories:

1. Family members
2. Personal friends
3. Social acquaintances
4. Business or professional contacts

Let's look at each group, one at a time, and start to weave our new network.

FAMILY MEMBERS

How big is your family? Really. You may be surprised! Do you tend to think of your family in terms of the immediate members: mother and dad, husband, wife, brothers and sisters, children? With networking we must consider the family group as the whole family, including grandparents, aunts, uncles, nephews, nieces and the whole family of in-laws on both sides.

These are the people that know you best, and hopefully, love you most. They're the natural place to start. If there is love lacking, networking may put the spark back into the relationship(s).

In her wonderful book ***The Aquarian Conspiracy,*** Marilyn Ferguson quotes from a Quaker newsletter:

"We will recognize that each person needs to nourish and be nourished by many persons, and we will not seek to restrict them through fear. We will know that we can only keep that which we set free....

"We recognize ourselves as members of the family of human beings. It is right, even necessary, to make yourselves available to one another in new loving, caring, and fulfilling ways – without the spectres of old guilts at loving widely."

What can family members do for you? They are the first knots in your net. They should be able to share your most intimate problems. They should also be counted on to provide support and praise. The family can lend more than support –

from their love, time, expertise, advice and money, to the proverbial borrowed lawn mower, depending on the closeness of the relative.

What can you do for your family? Follow the Golden Rule. Do for your whole family what you expect them to do for you. Remember that you are a knot in your own network and that like a net woven of cord, its strength is only that of the weakest knot.

There is still more you can do. As a networker you assume a more positive role and reach out to make sure all of your relatives are indeed knots in your net. This means a disciplined effort to maintain regular contacts. The contacts may take the form of visits, phone calls or letters.

In our ultra busy, two-job, shopping mall, fast food lifestyle, relatives – particularly older relatives – are often forgotten. Surely the telephone companies have tried to get you to "reach out and touch someone" and for many people, if you took away advertising mail and bills, there wouldn't be much left in their mailboxes.

Start your network with your family. Begin with your greeting card list and then expand. Since many in the family won't have formal calling cards to help you keep records, develop a 3" X 5" card, Rolodex® or computer file for names, addresses, phone numbers, and other profile information (more about specifics record keeping in chapter 8, *Your Networking Databank*). You'll want to include birthdays and other information that will help you strengthen your relationships.

Finally, as a disciplined networker, make a special effort to call or visit relatives whenever possible and practical. Recently we learned of a couple who went out of their way, on yearly vacation trips to Florida, to visit a distant cousin who lived alone. When she died, the attentive cousins were surprised to be the unexpected recipients of the lonely woman's modest estate. In her will she wrote, "These were the least of my relatives, but the most caring." The moral of the story is certainly not the financial gain, but rather the importance of attention, however minimal.

Our next step is to enlarge our network through personal relationships.

PERSONAL FRIENDS

As we move down our list of people with whom we're regularly involved you'll notice a decrease in intimacy. We are most intimate with family. Personal friends will follow family on our list. Included as personal friends are special people from groups such as co-workers, business associates, professionals and organization members who you might consider close to you.

Again, a greeting card list, or personal telephone or address book is a good place to start developing your network of personal friends. Review the names you now have. Can you separate the intimate friends from the casual acquaintances? Who would be likely to come to your aid when you're in trouble? To what degree of trouble?

Aside from developing your network of personal friends, this exercise may help you reevaluate your relationships with friends. Are there areas where you need to do some work, to put forth special efforts to enhance relationships?

Remember, you have to weave a strong network before you use it. With personal friends – *especially* with personal friends – you have to be exceedingly careful not to just *use* the friendship but to be equally ready to *commit* to the friendship. Networking is a two way street with each participant sharing.

You have to *be* a friend as well as have a friend.

Since your network of personal friends will also include people from other groups who are especially close to you, you will probably rely most often on this category of people. That's why it's so important to develop this list early and completely.

SOCIAL ACQUAINTANCES

Though less close to you than personal friends, social acquaintances play an extremely important role in networking. You might have an acquaintance you see daily at work or someone who you haven't seen in years. Both can play key roles in the networking process at crucial times.

All of us probably, at some time, have had a special need and also had an acquaintance who could satisfy or help with that need. The trick is to be able to identify the acquaintance – to be able to sometimes reach back, far back, into the past. This is where discipline plays such an important role in networking. To successfully use networking we must discipline ourselves to identify and record, to be able to pull up just the right name at just the right time to start our networking working.

BUSINESS COLLEAGUES & ACQUAINTANCES

These are the people you work with on a daily basis but who are not necessarily personal friends: employees, co-workers, superiors, clients, patients, customers, suppliers, business neighbors, and yes, even competitors.

This list may be the easiest to start because you've already had an existing need to maintain, in some form, a list of most of these people.

In his earlier book ***Network Your Net Worth,*** Tom Sullivan relates a scene described to him by Laura French. It is from an episode of the TV series "Lou Grant": "The reporters were all going on strike, and one by one the key characters came back to the newsroom to pick up the thing that was most meaningful. Billie Newman pulled a pair of high heeled sandals out of her desk drawer. Donovan took his special wooden coat hanger and Rossi, the dedicated reporter and the ultimate networker, seized his Rolodex® file. He actually clutched it to his chest as he left the newsroom. The message was quite clear: he'd be nothing without his sources, and he didn't want anyone else to use them in his absence. That's how it should be. We should all get to the point that if our offices caught fire, our file of names is the *one* thing we'd grab and take with us. It would be all we would need to start rebuilding..."

Whether it be your Rolodex®, 3" X 5" cards, a collection of business cards or a sophisticated computer program, your list of names – your database – is the starting point for your network and for networking.

3

Networking Skills

What makes a good networker?

Is networking really for you?

Good networkers have a lot of things in common. That's not to say that anybody can't be a good networker – but if you're lacking some of these skills or traits and you are still committed to networking, you will have to work a little harder to attain the success you want.

TEN CHARACTERISTICS OF GOOD NETWORKERS

1. Assertive. Networkers are reach-out people. People eager to meet other people. People who are comfortable in gatherings. People who are comfortable with themselves and secure. People who want to like other people and want other people to like them. People who are not afraid to initiate contacts.

2. Good Communication Skills. Networkers are good verbal and written communicators. They can translate ideas into both easy-to-read and easy-to-understand language. They can put their thoughts into words quickly. They tend to use shorter words, shorter sentences and shorter paragraphs to get their point across.

3. Good Listener Skills. In addition to being able to communicate in an outward manner, networkers have to be skilled in the reverse situation and be good listeners. Remembering that networking is a connecting system, the communications forces are two-way. For assertive people, the tendency is often to talk *to*, rather than to talk *with*. When you want something from somebody you have to listen to them very carefully. How they say something might be just as important as what they say.

4. Inquisitive. It was Rudyard Kipling who wrote, "I have five servants, tried and true. Their names are what and when and where and why and who." A good starting point for networkers. But you must go beyond Kiplings's five questions. You have to be inquisitive about people, places, situations and things. How do you network with things? Well, you really don't, but things often lead you to special people.

If, for instance, you read a particularly interesting book or see an exciting new product, you may want to network with the author, inventor or supplier of the new publication or product.

5. An Avid Reader. International Paper Company studied the reading habits of 100 young business people who were members of management training programs and considered likely to become executives.

They found that these people read an average of three magazines and twelve newspapers a week.

An identical survey among 100 company vice-presidents between the ages of 45 and 50 found, that in a single week, these busy people found time to read three and a half magazines and 15 newspapers.

Similar studies show that successful architects, teachers, scientists, salespeople and politicians read more than their less successful counterparts. The point we make here is that as networkers keep on reading, their careers will move upward.

6. Honest. We'll make the assumption that everyone reading this book is honest. In networking it's the often small nuances of honesty that can play a key role. Do you exaggerate? Do you keep your promises? Do you make promises you can't keep? Do you respect confidences? Do you gossip – using information from your network? Do you bribe? (Don't ask *us* for the definition...you'll know it if you do.)

Even though any of us may unintentionally slip into one of these situations, the penalties are high. Getting caught can destroy some or all of your valuable network.

The news of misdeeds seems to travel through networks faster than the news of good deeds. (Maybe we should put quote marks around that sentence and call it Sullivan and Erdman's law.)

7. Creative. Creativity plays an enormously important role in networking. It applies to finding people and information, to problem solving, to research, to promoting yourself, to unusual uses of the tools of networking, and to organizing and refining the network you've built.

Many people believe that you are born creative, but we challenge that notion. We believe that just as people exercise their muscles and become stronger, you can exercise you brain and become more creative.

One of the concepts Ken promotes is his "AQ" or "awareness quotient," an expression he came up with some twenty or more years ago. The awareness quotient is, unlike your IQ with specific gradings, a non-specific yardstick of how aware you are of things related to and of importance to your personal needs. Some people look at something and see only its surface. Others look at the same thing and see something of value or potential value. One person looks at a chocolate chip cookie and sees someting to eat. Another looks at the cookie and sees the opportunity for a new business.

People can learn to be more creative. It's not an overnight phenomenon, but like TV preacher Robert Schuller says, "Inch by inch, anything's a cinch."

8. Generous. Didn't somebody say something about *getting*? To be successful, networking has to be a combination of both giving and getting. We're not talking about giving as in, "I did you a favor and you owe me a favor in return." We're talking about free-will giving, casting your bread upon the waters giving.

In his wonderful book, ***Try Giving Yourself Away,*** David Dunn describes the event that led to his achieving a "giving himself away" lifestyle. The book grew out of an article with the same title that appeared anonymously in ***Forbes*** magazine and was also reprinted in an abbreviated version in ***Reader's Digest.***

While making one of his monthly trips on the Twentieth Century Limited, a famous New York to Chicago train of bygone days, Dunn wondered where the New York bound and Chicago bound trains passed in the night. It occurred to him that this "passing" had the makings of an intriguing advertisement. For Dunn, this wasn't just an idle thought – he acted upon it.

He wrote to the New York Central Lines and gave them the idea with no strings attached. Soon he received a letter with the information that the trains were scheduled to pass near a small town nines miles west of Buffalo.

Later he received another letter telling him that the railroad was going to use his idea for a picture on their next calendar. The headline would be: "Where the Centuries Pass." The photo showed the trains passing in the night. And the rest is history. The calendar was widely distributed in both this country and in Europe, and to collectors of railroading memorabilia it's a prized possession.

David Dunn, having reaped so much pleasure from giving things away, devoted the rest of his life to giving himself away. You too, can and should try giving yourself away. You can give with small acts as well as things. A piece of information, a small courtesy, a recipe, a greeting card, a magazine clipping...all are without monetary value but all are cherished by the recipient.

9. Disciplined. There's that word from our definition, *disciplined acquaintanceship*.

We don't use the word discipline in its harshest sense, but rather as a combination of several words – perhaps words like organized, active and assertive. Disciplined networkers make a habit of updating and organizing the names in their network. They work at networking every day. They are assertive in their contacts; there is nothing passive about disciplined networkers. They keep good records and use the many tools available to them.

In later chapters you'll read about some super networkers. Look closely and you'll probably find the tell-tale signs of good discipline in every story.

10. Good Natured. Yes, networking is serious business. Yes, you do it to achieve success. But we sincerely believe that networking should be a fun process. With some networkers there is a sense of personal seriousness, often coupled with a sense of urgency that becomes a turn-off.

You can (and should) take your networking seriously, but be careful not to take yourself too seriously.

Have *fun* networking yourself to success!

4

Knots In Your Network

Identifying the special people who will lead you to success

Your network, as its very name suggests, is like a net. Imagine it being woven and held together by a series of interconnecting knots.

Each knot represents a person you can call on and use to help gain success. Most of the people (knots) will play minor rolls in your quest. They're good people to know and they may come in handy someday.

And then there are special knots. A special knot in your network is someone extraordinary – someone who has unique knowledge, specific skills, special know-how, distinctive talent or exceptional contacts.

Special people are the people you call on most frequently for help. They're the people on your auto-dialing list. They're the people whose addresses you have committed to memory.

Special knots can be neatly classified for the ways in which they can be helpful. Other authors have named and described these exceptional people, but there is not a consensus as to terms. So we'll name and describe our very own special knots using our own vocabulary.

THE PRO'S

These are the people you call on regularly to get every day jobs done most efficiently and often at the lowest prices. They're people with whom you are comfortable. Your Pro's are probably already in your telephone or address book or on your Rolodex®.

Pro's include your lawyer, your doctor, your stockbroker, your barber, your handy man your hair stylist – almost anybody whose services you use consistently.

For a variety of reasons you may have to look for new Pro's. Here's where you network. You ask other Pro's for recommendations. Who do they use and why? If you're comfortable with the people you ask you'll probably be comfortable with the people they suggest.

THE LIBRARIANS

Ask them anything. They are the people who have the answers to just about anything you want to know. Librarians are often intellectuals, but need not be. They come from all walks of life, and their vast storehouses of knowledge tend to be multifaceted. This is probably because Librarians are usually diverse readers with a menu that includes books, trade journals, magazines, newsletters and newspapers.

Another characteristic of Librarians is that they enjoy challenges. Ask them a question that they can't answer, or can't answer completely, and they will go out of their way to get your answer...with no obligation. They do it for the sheer joy of solving your problem.

MENTORS

If you are looking for success, why not emulate successful people? That's what Mentors are all about.

They're the people in your life who are often (though not necessarily) more successful than you. People who set an example – who set the standard for you in family life, social life, in business or in your profession. They're people you look up to and respect. Mentors can be called on for special needs because you probably have established a deeper personal relationship with them.

SUPERKNOTS

You just can't get along without them. Superknots are those very special friends that can seemingly get you anything you need, know anything you want to know or find anything you need to find.

Superknots are themselves, super networkers. They seem to know any and everybody who's worth knowing. But you have to be careful with Superknots. You don't want to over use them and wear out your welcome. Another characteristic of Superknots is their very long memories. They're quick to do favors but long remember the favor...that's why they are so effective. They have a long list of people who they can ask for favors on *your* behalf.

ADVOCATES

We borrowed this term from internationally known speaker and writer, Murray Raphel of Atlantic City, New Jersey.

He borrowed it from ad man extraordinaire Ray Considine of California, who borrowed it from California training workshop promoter, Ray Cusato, who says he borrowed from friend and co-workshop leader Walter Geyer.

Here's how Murray describes an Advocate: "Someone who tells everyone else to buy from you. The Advocate is someone who is so happy with what they are buying from you that they become a disciple.

"When new people come into town and are looking to buy a particular product, this person brings them directly to you and says, 'I want you to take care of these folks the same way you take care of me!' That is what an advocate is – someone who goes around town bringing customers to you."

For the purposes of networking, our Advocates won't strictly be involved in the sales process. Our Advocates are those people who go out of their way, often way out of their way – on your behalf – without expecting anything in return.

Advocates like and respect you and they're willing to tell other people what they think about you. An Advocate may be your closest friend or your best customer or client, or someone just a bit further removed. An important aspect of networking is to identify your Advocates and cultivate them.

TOMORROWS

Here's a "just for fun" group. They don't fit into the traditional concept of the knots in your network. You won't have them listed in your files. In fact, you haven't even met them. Tomorrows are the knots that *will* be in your network... tomorrow. But they are just as important (and sometime more important) than knots you already have in your network. They are the people you'll meet by chance that will unexpectedly be of great help to you. You always have to be on the lookout for great tomorrows!

Tomorrows are short lived. As soon as you've met them and recognized their potential you put them in your files and they'll turn from Tomorrows into another category.

Now that you have identified all of the people in your network, classified the special people and recognized the opportunities to use them, you're ready to move on.

5

How To Use Your Network

To network your way to success

OK. Now you've got a network in place. What are you going to do with it?

Good question.

At a recent wedding reception, someone who learned Ken was working on this book asked, "How can you fill an entire book just on the subject of meeting people?" Ken's first impulse was to say, "Buy the book and find out." But that wouldn't have been good networking etiquette. (Talk about the sale *after* you've made the contact.)

The real answer is that networking isn't just about meeting people. It's about gathering information, locating sources, attracting support, getting help for projects, making sales, tapping sources of influence, finding jobs, seeking advice, gaining exposure... the list goes on and on.

For each of the objectives of networking there are different ways and different tools to reach your goals. Meeting people – or schmoozing – is just one technique to use to make personal contacts. (And no, we wouldn't want to try to write an entire book on schmoozing.)

NETWORKING FOR INFORMATION

Several years ago a Rotarian friend of Ken's, James Lacey of Cookville, Tennessee, was interested in purchasing a candy company in Ken's locality. Jim needed more information on the company – information that was perhaps not revealed in the formal documents and literature available to him.

Ken is part of Jim's network, so Jim called and asked Ken what he knew about the company. Did he have any contacts that could be of help? Surprisingly, one of Ken's superknots, Tom Reinhart, of Reading, Pennsylvania, sold packaging to candy companies...and the company Jim was interested in was one of Tom's good customers. Tom was able to provide Jim with a lot of helpful information.

During a mutual fund board meeting, the fund's counsel mentioned that he was having trouble getting information about stock that was held in a company in the South. He complained that the problem was with a clerk in the courthouse.

Guess what? Ken has a friend who is a judge in the district where the company is located. He called him.

"Judge," he said, "I have a problem and I need your help. (See Chapter 18, *The Nine Magic Words of Networking*.) Can you do me a favor and make a phone call to see if *you* can get my answer?"

It's amazing how much influence a judge has in his own courthouse.

These are ideal examples of networking for information.

NETWORKING DIRECTORIES

One of our summer interns, Susan Tomkin, from Penn State University, put together a networking directory for her fellow College of Business Administration students. Her preface to the directory had this to say about networking for information: "Everyone that you come in contact with is a potential source of useful information. In turn, you are also a source of information to everyone you meet." She then went on to explain why the networking directory would be valuable and gave ten ways it could be used.

Most organizations publish member directories although they don't necessarily call them networking directories. Susan's directory went beyond just listing names, addresses and phone numbers. She included sports interests, hobbies, other extracurricular activities, work experiences, internships and career goals and objectives.

Susan also helped with the proofreading and editing of this book. She has since graduated from Penn State is now the Production Assistant with a Philadelphia advertising agency.

DEVELOPING SUPPLIERS

Finding sources of supply for both products and services is one of the most common uses for networkers. Where can I get my car fixed? Who can resurface my driveway? Who can I rely on to supply the flowers for my daughter's wedding? You want the best service (with a smile) at a reasonable price. Someone you can trust to do a good job...on time.

Turn to your network. Ask a few of your Pro's about who they have used for similar jobs and in similar situations. Most of the time you'll find just the right supplier. (Using networking there will be far more winners than losers.)

NETWORKING AND SELLING

Salespeople are among the largest and most active group of networkers. If there is one word that describes the difference between a peddler and professional salesperson, it's *networking*.

We see peddlers as people who make a lot of cold calls, who rely on averages – if you make enough calls you'll sell something. The networker, on the other hand, works to get appointments, gathers information about the company and the buyer and may even get an Advocate to intercede.

The networking salesperson has an organized business card cataloging system. His or her Rolodex® is bulging with entries. Their computers are brimming with names, addresses, phone numbers fax numbers, key contacts and other important information. There's probably a fax handy and perhaps a cellular phone. The networking salesperson uses all of the tools available to gain that extra edge and extra sale. Selling is perhaps the one of the primary uses for networking, and networking is the prime resource of selling.

See Chapter 26, *Putting it All Together: Networking and Selling* for more in depth discussion of networking and sales.

JOB HUNTING

Pat Payer-Kane, Senior Vice President at International Merchandise Concepts in Calabasas, CA, told us of an interview she had for a job as a sales manager. She mentioned that the first question she was asked was, "Who do you know in the industry?"

Many people are hired specifically for who and how many people they know in their particular field or industry – for the size of their business network. The bigger your network the better, when it comes to job hunting.

In a later chapter we'll take a look at some specific ways networking can help you find a new or better job.

ATTRACTING SUPPORT

Most of us, at one time or another, have had a cause which needed outside support to be successful. It could be a project at work, a charitable endeavor, or a political position.

This is where you reach out to the Advocates in your network. They know you, they trust you and they are most likely to support both you and your cause.

SEEKING ADVICE

This is an aspect of networking that many people overlook. We all need advice on occasion, and our network is the first place to start. We can turn to our family and also go outside. Here again is a situation where you'll probably rely on Advocates in your network who will be both honest and unbiased.

Advice is needed on all levels. For example, young company presidents are a lonely lot. They need advice but often don't have someone they can trust or rely on for unbiased help. It was probably this need that spawned the Young Presidents

Organization (YPO), a place where young company presidents could gather to seek advice and share ideas from others with similar experiences and similar problems.

Now that you've seen some of the opportunities to use your network to network your way to success, let's activate it, and learn how to reach out to the names you've collected.

6

Networking: It's As Easy As 1, 2, 3, (4)

I know someone who knows someone who knows just the right someone

It's been said that with networking you can reach almost anybody you might need for help with only three phone calls. And that means...anybody!

You've must be kidding! Anybody?

How far can you really carry this networking stuff? Could you possible network to the President?

How *about* the President? Do you think you could get to the Oval Office with three phone calls?

These are some of the questions that came up during a luncheon with a couple of friends while we were in the process of writing this book and testing ideas for material to be included.

"Let's play a game," Tom suggested. "You two pick some people that you think might be hard to get to and then we'll all rack our brains, or better yet, search our networking files (from memory) and see how close we can really network to reach the 'toughies.'"

"OK," said one of the players. "Let's try the President. How close can we come?"

After just a little thought, this challenge turned out to be much easier than any of our little group expected. The closest friend of one of us had a brother who was an ambassador to a major nation and known by the President on a first name basis. We all agreed that there was at least a chance that we could get to the President through him in three phone calls.

Next Mikhail Gorbachev. Impossible! Certainly not in three phone calls. But wait. Tom Sullivan remembered that Minnesota Governor Rudy Perpich had been personally responsible for bringing Gorbachev to Minnesota in 1990. If he got to Governor Perpich in two phone calls perhaps the Governor could get to his new friend Mikhail Gorbachev.

"Come on, give us a really tough one," Ken challenged.

"OK, wise guy," came the reply from one of the group. "Try *The Pope!*"

Dead silence.

And then Ken came up with the solution. He had a Mentor in his personal network who is an intimate friend of John Paul II, and was, at that very time, working on a special project for the Pope.

Wow. You really might reach almost anybody in just three phone calls. Not always, of course. But we bet that those of you who develop your networks and aggressively pursue them will have a much better than average chance. You'll be that much closer to reaching almost anybody you need in just a couple of phone calls when you start with someone in your network.

THE FOUR-MULA FOR SUCCESS

We discovered this remarkably effective formula for success in the book ***The Great Brain Robbery*** by Ray Considine & Murray Raphel.

In their Great (and we mean *Great* with a capital "G" – you really should read it) book, the authors propose the Eleventh Commandment. It goes like this: Thou Shalt Steal Every Idea Thou Can Find...and Make It Thine Own.

So we took their advice and stole the Four-mula for Success. Only, we're not keeping it for ourselves...we're *sharing it with you.*

A banker in Nebraska tried this formula and made an $800,000 transaction.

A small retail store tried this formula and did an extra $5,000 in business at a cost of just $100.

Another banker made a phone call and sold a $100,000 certificate of deposit during a coffee break.

These stories are the result of Considine and Raphel's four step, easy-to-follow guaranteed way of increasing business. How did the authors get these stories? How do they know their Four-mula really works? Hundreds of people who have attended their seminars and who have read their book write in, phone in or mention their personal successes after adopting the Four-mula.

We think their Four-mula is not only a formula for success but also an excellent networking formula. The Four-mula for Success requires only that you set aside part of your day to contact customers, prospects, patients, clients, friends or others in your network who can help you succeed.

To begin you must agree that it *is* important to set aside a certain portion of each day for new business or contacts. Spend the rest of the day with usual routine matters which involve keeping your present customers, patients or clients happy. If you agree to set aside up to 20 minutes each day, the formula will work for you.

There are four different ways. You can employ one from each category, four from one or *any* combination of four. The result is always the same – more business. Here's what Considine and Raphel suggest.

Four Notes

Write four notes a day to people you want to influence, to people in your network or to people you want in your network. These can be thank you notes, "newsy" notes, notes with clippings from magazines or newspapers on subjects of interest to the receiver, a greeting card, a note of congratulations, or a note of appreciation. You can probably think of even more reasons to write.

Pay attention now. We're not talking about letters, we're talking about *notes*. Hand-written notes work best, but a typewritten note is better than none. Those handy little "sticky" notes are great to attach to articles and clippings.

Finding reasons to write to people is not as hard as you may think. Just scan your local papers and you'll come up with some good reasons. A review of your networking files will reveal birthdays and other relative information for triggering a note. While reading magazines you'll come across articles and items to clip. (Remember, good networkers are good readers.)

How effective are these notes? Consider how little *personal* mail the average person receives. Consider also that much of the mail people receive is *negative* in nature. (How often do bills appear in your daily mail?) The four notes leaving *your* desk are going to be *positive*. Now you can better understand how much your personal notes will mean to those who receive them.

Four Telephone Calls

This is the same as four notes. Only on the phone. You will be amazed at the positive reactions. Ask anyone you know how often they've received a positive phone call from someone they did business with.

Rarely.

Now, imagine the reaction when you call, say your name, your company's name and, "Is this Mrs. Jones? Good morning. I'm calling to say thank you for doing business with us. We appreciate your business and want you to know if there is any other way we can help you in the future, we would certainly like to hear from you..."

Mrs. Jones will probably call back to see if you really work there or if your call was a practical joke. Who ever heard of a company calling to say *thank you*?

Here's another true-life story from the ***Great Brain Robbery***. A banker in a small town in Nebraska heard the four phone call technique explained at a seminar given by the authors. He immediately started a system of calling four business accounts every day. He would go through the "loans approved" list, pick up the phone, call, and thank the account for doing business with the bank.

One day he called to thank the owner of a business who had borrowed a substantial amount of money. The owner was in conference and was called away by his secretary, who assumed that *any* call from the bank was urgent. The businessman's reaction was astonishment. The only reason the banker was calling him was to *thank* him for the loan? He had assumed that the bank had reconsidered and decided *not* to give him the money!

He was reassured but did need convincing that the phone call was nothing more than a thank you. He then asked the banker to hold the phone for a minute. He returned with the message, "This is your lucky day. I'm in a meeting with a new business coming to town. I just told him about this phone call. He said you're the kind of bank he wants to deal with. Send a messenger over for his check for $800,000."

The banker nearly fainted.

And that's just one of the many stories we could tell about the power of those four phone calls a day.

Four Personal Contacts

This should be easy for salespeople. It's a little tougher for those who don't always get away from the office. But most of you can do it on a fairly regular basis when you consider all of the people you do see in a day beyond the office or house. It may be when you're shopping, eating out, at church, at the country club, while pursuing hobbies or visiting.

What's the difference between just seeing people and making a networking contact? The personal networking contact comes from a disciplined effort to start or enhance an acquaintanceship. Often we're too casual when meeting new people for the first time. OK, we've met, so what? The networking contact is a *positive, active* contact. You make the contact with the expectation of something happening. You cause something to happen by being especially friendly, offering extra smiles, being inquisitive, handing out your card (more on this later) or by conveying a genuine interest in the person you meet.

While checking into the Hyatt Hotel on the waterfront in Baltimore, Ken chatted with the front desk person, Virginia, while she was registering him. She noticed that Ken had a couple of old metal bottle openers in his hand. "What do you do with the old bottle openers?" Virginia asked. Ken told her of his hobby of collecting old imprinted advertising specialties and that someone had just handed him the openers. Virginia then told him about a collection of old imprinted pencils which had belonged to her father. She said she had always hoped that she could find someone to give them to who would appreciate their historic value. "I'll bring them when I come to work tomorrow morning," she said, "and you can pick them up when you check out." True to her word, Virginia brought in the pencils the next morning. (The Hyatt Hotel chain really hires the nicest people.)

It is a great collection. Virginia did indeed find someone who appreciates the historic value of those old advertising pencils.

Four Sales Calls

From ***The Great Brain Robbery***: "Every time two people meet, a sale is made." True. But only if one of them knows it.

The exchange might not be for something tangible. It could be the selling of a concept, an idea, or the realization of a job you set out to do. A completed transaction.

If completing four sales calls poses a problem on a daily basis, remember, you can mix and match items from the Fourmula. If you can't make four sales calls a day, make up the difference with notes or phone calls.

The greeting, the talking to and the contacting of a minimum number of people every day to make four sales calls is *not* difficult. What makes it a bit more challenging? Each of the four sales calls brings you closer to your goals each day. Set your sales goals. You will achieve them with networking.

You see, networking can be as easy as 1, 2, 3, (4).

7

Networking's Two Most Important Words

"Thank You"

It seems to us appropriate that we end Part One of our book – the part that deals with the basic concepts of networking – with some words about networking's two most important words: "Thank You."

Networking is basically an active pursuit. We spend most of our networking time developing and maintaining our network. We actively "work" our network by person-to-person contacts, by mail, by telephone, through newsletters, publicity and other techniques.

ACTIVE VERSUS PASSIVE NETWORKING

The often overlooked function of networking is a passive function. That function is to say, "Thank You." Think about it. When was the last time a business or professional person sent you a "Thank You" message?

We buy (and probably most of you have, too) houses, cars, jewelry, major appliances, stereo equipment and a host of other things with big price tags...but we seldom receive "Thank You" notes or letters for our purchases.

How about all of the times you have helped someone, perhaps as a direct result of a networking situation. Or the special efforts you've made in your business or profession that were really above and beyond. Were these missed opportunities for a "Thank You?" Don't *you* miss the opportunity to express appreciation for special services or favors.

THE CUSTOMER IS KING

The business headlines of the '90's scream, "SERVICE, SERVICE, SERVICE! The Customer is King!" If that's really true, why not honor the king (or queen)? Why not say "Thanks" to those in your network?

Because so many people don't send them, the impact of "Thank You" letters, notes, or cards is fantastic.

Recently, we opened an additional business bank account. We are old and faithful customers, but it seems that the bank took us for granted. We did not receive any kind of "Thank You."

One of us spent several hours preparing a speech for a service club, left his wife at home alone for dinner, and drove 60 miles round-trip to make the presentation. Although the speech was well received, there was no "Thank You" phone call or letter – no follow up at all.

Two months ago the last payment of a mortgage was made. That's a very important event in anyone's life – but again, you guessed it...no "Thank You" from the bank.

"THANK YOU" AS A NETWORKING TOOL

By contrast, when Ken Erdman's son and daughter-in-law joined a new church, Ken and his wife Sue received a note expressing the minister's appreciation of their attendance at the occasion – with an added message, asking them to visit the church again. They did. A month later Ken and Sue's two grandchildren were baptized in the same church. And again, they received a personal letter about their attending that very special celebration. For a second time, the minister didn't miss the opportunity to extend yet another invitation to come to a service...and to again say "Thank You."

Every check we receive for a column from one of our newsletter clients says "Thank You," handwritten in the lower left hand memo block. One of our suppliers writes to thank us for paying our bills so promptly. Can you just imagine how good that makes us feel?

ADVANTAGES AND EXAMPLES

You can begin to see the advantages of "Thank You" networking. It has impact, it's very personal, it helps build a continuing relationship with your network and it can be a form of subtle salesmanship.

The telephone is perhaps the quickest and most convenient way to say "Thank You." For important "Thank You" mail with high impact, the letter is your best bet. If you want to make your message highly personal, the note is the answer. If you're pressed for time, a "Thank You" greeting card is quick and appropriate. A simple way to say "Thank You" is with a postcard. In some cases, where there has been a substantial favor given, a small gift is in order.

CONCEPT VERSUS COPY

The really important aspect of using the words "Thank You" is the sincerity of the writer. If you read this chapter but get into a "Thank You" mode only as a copy style, you may be missing the point.

The words "Thank You" reflect appreciation. For these magic words to work the writer or caller must *sincerely* convey a sense of appreciation.

Could it be that the people in your network really *are* king and queen?

We think so!

Part Two

Casting Your Net

Developing Your Network

8

Your Networking Databank

Making deposits and withdrawals

In today's marketing jargon, you'll frequently hear about database marketing. Direct marketers invented the concept specifically for direct mail purposes. Lately telemarketing has also benefited from database marketing. Your database is basically your mailing list. The list could (and should) be expanded to include more than just the names and addresses of customers and prospects. More sophisticated databases include demographic details to help pinpoint specific buying or lifestyle habits that can easily be targeted.

You can be sure when you get a direct mail solicitation or your telephone rings with a special offer, the selection of your particular name wasn't accidental. Marketers with well-honed databases know more about you than you would imagine.

DATABANK – WHAT DOES IT MEAN?

Perhaps your database would more properly be called your data*bank* – a place where you make deposits and withdrawals of information and earn networking interest. In this chapter, we'll be referring to your database as your databank. The databank is your personal collection of names and associated information that you maintain and use to "work" your network. Just as marketers rely on their databases for better returns from their mailings and telemarketing efforts, so too will networkers get better results based on the quality of the information in their personal databanks.

MORE THAN JUST NAMES

Everyone has some way of keeping track of names, addresses and telephone numbers. The databank concept goes a little farther, incorporating additional information *about* the person, as well as how to contact them. You will want to include information about hobbies, memberships, family, interests, etc. After you record your contact's name and address information, you can add this additional data which will be very helpful in your networking efforts.

Your databank could be – depending on how extensive and important your network is – an address and phone book, an organized collection of business cards, information on 3" X 5" cards, a Rolodex® filing system, a sophisticated computer program or a combination of any or all of these elements.

BUILDING YOUR DATABANK

To get started you must first build your databank. You have to decide which system or systems of storage and retrieval will work best for you.

If you are really serious about networking (and we hope that by the time you finish this book you will be) you'll probably go beyond a simple telephone and address book to store your data.

Although the computer is the ultimate databank, many networkers do a great job with the other databank systems mentioned: 3" X 5" cards, a Rolodex®, a computer program, a system for cataloging business cards or again, a combination of all of these.

3" X 5" CARDS

The advantage of 3" X 5" cards is that they provide plenty of room for information. Plus there are file drawers and indexing systems available for their organization and storage. Index cards are also a very convenient size to work with and don't cause any eye strain. The disadvantage is that much of the information on the cards will be taken from business cards, creating a duplicate effort.

THE ROLODEX®

In *The Harvey Mackay Rolodex® Network Builder*, Harvey Mackay, author of ***How to Swim With the Sharks Without Being Eaten Alive*** and ***Beware the Naked Man Who Offers You His Shirt***, suggests that the word *Rolodex®* is one of the most important words in the English language. He credits the 6,500 names in his Rolodex® files with much of his success in his business and social life.

The Rolodex® brand rotary filing system for names, addresses and telephone numbers has revolutionized basic information storage systems. It seems you see the familiar Rolodex® card holders on almost every desk in every office. This system has the advantage of easy card removal and replacement for quickly making new entries, adding entries or correcting entries.

Space is available on both sides of Rolodex® cards for most of the information networkers will need. Many people are now using a type of business cards which are sized and die-cut to fit Rolodex® files. The system also provides a selection of models with the ability to store huge numbers of cards.

In addition to mechanical Rolodex® files, the manufacturer also provides a line of battery-operated and portable electronic Rolodex® files, perfect for traveling and on-the-road use.

BUSINESS CARD FILING SYSTEM

This is a simple and convenient system which utilizes the business cards you collect from networking encounters. It requires a business card porta-file that holds approximately 96 cards, and a three-ring binder with clear vinyl sheets that have pockets for individual business cards. Both of these items are readily available from stationery and department stores.

The system that Tom Sullivan likes to use is to mark down pertinent information on the back of a card as soon as he receives it. He then puts the card in a sleeve in his business card file. He begins his filing at the back of the porta-file. This way, his most current cards are always at the front. His file is truly portable, as he carries it in his brief case and works from it at the office, on the road and at home.

The porta-file has the advantage of a visual display of the people with whom he has most recently been in contact. A quick flip through his file refreshes his memory and reminds him of necessary follow-ups.

When Tom's porta-file fills up, he transfers the cards to the vinyl sheets in his three-ring notebook. Now Tom files the sheets, with appropriate dividers, according to occupation or other descriptive classification. Again, as with the porta-file, he has the advantage of reviewing cards quickly by glancing through the pages of his binders.

COMPUTER DATABANKS

The most sophisticated databank is the computer. Not only can you store and retrieve information with ease, but you have an infinite variety of ways to manipulate the information you store.

Depending upon the software you use, you can organize your databank according to how you would like to view or print it. You can electronically earmark an entry based on several criteria: the relationship to you and your network (friend, family, customer, prospect), geographical location, occupation, birthday, family information (children's names, wedding anniversary, siblings, parents), memberships and other activities.

You can designate which records you want to print out for mailing labels or reports, and only those particularly designated names will print. Most software used for name storage will allow you, with a modem, to automatically dial the phone numbers in your computer.

Computer portability has increasingly become an asset to many networkers. Many new models of pocket or briefcase computers with increased capabilities for information storage and even word processing abilities have come into the market.

MAKING DEPOSITS

Once you've built your databank, you will have to decide what you want to include in it. Certainly you'll have the typical information: name, address, phone and fax numbers. You can also add where and when you met a person, the person's birth date, information about their family, hobbies or other interests. If the contact has a secretary or assistant you will want that name. You can also note when you made the last contact with that person or when you should make the next contact. This data can all be recorded on your 3" X 5" cards, on the back of business cards, on your Rolodex® or in your computer. The amount of information in any databank will depend on how serious the individual networker is.

WITHDRAWALS FROM YOUR DATABANK

When making phone calls or writing letters, you can and should use information from your databank. In a typical phone call you can address a prospect's secretary by name. This will surely improve your chances of getting through to that person or having the person call you back. Knowing a person's sports interest, hobbies, family information and other particulars gives you clues as to what to say to get a good conversation going and to impress your listener with your particular interest in them.

If you collect birthday information about people in your network you can call or send a greeting card on the appropriate date. Again this builds a more personal relationship.

DATABANK SECURITY

Just as real banks have vaults and security guards, so too, should you takes steps to insure the security of your most valuable networking tool. You should store your 3" X 5" card files, your Rolodex® files, your business card files or your backup computer disk in a fire-retardant file case or safe. Just consider the predicament you would be in if you were to lose hundreds or thousands of networking contact information!

YOU ARE AS GOOD AS YOUR DATABANK

No matter how hard you pursue networking, how dynamic your personality or how many friends you have, without a well organized databank your results will suffer.

Your databank – used in your office, on the road and at home – will prove to be a most valuable networking tool.

9

Tele-Networking

Tapping the power of your phone

Of all the tools for networking, your telephone is the one you'll use most often. The telephone call is fast, direct, personal and inexpensive.

For all of its advantages, however, telephone communications are not without problems.

It's estimated that the average business executive wastes five to seven hours each week playing "phone tag" (not being able to complete calls), taking calls that should have been screened and being involved in unnecessarily long calls. AT&T estimates that for every thirty calls you make, fewer than eight are completed on the first try.

Knowing both the advantages and disadvantages of telephone communications gives networkers the opportunity to maximize the use of the telephone in their networking endeavors.

GETTING STARTED IN TELE-NETWORKING

Before you pick up the phone to make your first tele-networking call, there is some homework to be done. Being prepared to make effective calls plays an important role in the success of the calls you make. Let's look together at some of the preliminary steps to tele-networking.

THE TELEPHONE WORKSTATION

The place where you use your telephone – whether at home or at the office or both – should be set up to make the most efficient use of your time. *You* don't want to be the one to waste five to seven hours a week on your phone.

First, make sure you will be comfortable. Sit in a good chair have and your telephone within easy reach. In a "Phone Power" seminar by noted telephone consultant, George Walther, we learned to use extra long cords on our phones. This gives us the latitude to move around and get files or other material without having to put the phone down and interrupt the conversation. We also learned that if you are going to spend a large amount of continuous time on the phone, you may want to consider the possibility of a headset to free up both of your hands and to relieve the physical burden of continually holding the handset.

Although a popular phone accessory, speaker phones serve best for calls involving more than one person at either end of the conversation. Using a speaker phone during conversation between only two people can be annoying to the other person because of a hollow sound and extraneous noise.

At your tele-networking station (which is most probably your desk) be sure to have plenty of pencils, pens, paper and telephone answering slips readily available.

Now you may be saying to yourselves, "Hey this is elementary, who needs to be told?" But how many times have *you* heard someone say, "Just a minute...let me find a piece of paper." You'll also save time if you have all of your reference materials, including phone directories, within easy reach. We're probably all guilty, at one time or another, of not being prepared.

The most important thing to have readily available is your database. It might be your computer, your business card files, telephone/address books or 3" x 5" cards. You'll rely on your database for making outgoing calls and you'll need it to promptly record information from your calls.

PREPARING FOR YOUR OUTGOING CALLS

Before you start dialing you should prepare for your outgoing calls. Know what you are going to talk about, know what you are going to say and know what results you expect from the call. Do your research before the call. Look up and have handy any background information you may need. It sometimes helps, particularly if your conversation will be lengthy and detailed, to have a short written outline of the points you want to cover.

Take a few minutes to think through what you are going to say. Establish a mental picture of the person you'll be speaking with. Some communications experts suggest that you look at yourself in the mirror. This will give you some idea of what the other person is going to visualize when you call.

Do you have a happy face? Do you *reflect* a happy face – the face of someone who is going to sound friendly on the phone?

MANAGING YOUR OUTGOING CALLS

The beginning of your networking calls will be the process of getting through to the right people. With most calls this shouldn't be a problem. With some calls, however, you'll have to be pleasantly persistent, asking questions until you get the person you want.

When introducing yourself, enunciate clearly, spelling your name if there is any possibility of confusion. We recommend introducing yourself first and then asking for the party you want to reach.

Keep a smile in your voice. Try to convince the person called, with your personality and attitude, that you want to be friendly. The chances are that the listener will similarly respond.

Outline in more detail who you are and what you want. Don't be afraid to use someone as a reference if it might help you to get through to a hard-to-reach person.

Keep your business networking conversations brief. Many phone conversations are much longer than necessary because of wasted words and thoughts. The recipient of your call probably has a limited interest span that you won't want to exceed.

Control the conversation. Be confident. Don't be afraid to ask for help. (See chapter 18, "The Nine Magic Words of networking.") Don't be afraid of possible rejection – nobody bats a thousand. Convince yourself that if this phone call doesn't work, the next one will.

The exceptions to these suggestions are for social networking phone calls, during which your conversations will probably be longer and less structured.

MANAGING YOUR INCOMING CALLS

Since networking is two-way communication, the incoming call is just as important as the outgoing call.

We recommend that you answer your phone after the second ring. Some may disagree, but the extra ring gives the person called those few important seconds to mentally prepare for answering the call.

Your phone answering voice should have the same smile and radiate the same enthusiasm as your calling voice. You should project an image of appreciation of the call and interest in the caller.

Just as you were ready to take notes during your outgoing calls, you should be equally prepared for note taking during incoming calls. If you are not sure of the correct spelling of names, don't guess, ask the caller to spell them out. Don't rely on your memory for details – write them down.

FOLLOW-UP AND FOLLOW-THROUGH

One of the most important elements of tele-networking is doing what you promised to do...and doing it promptly. If you promise to call back at a certain time, don't put it off, keep your promise. If you promise to send something, send it – promptly.

Follow up on your networking calls. It may be helpful to make a record in your databank as a memory jogger to show when you last talked to someone. A sales axiom suggests that the best potential for new sales is from existing or old customers. The same holds true for networking. Keep your network active and your network will keep you active.

ANSWERING MACHINES

In the 1980's answering machines were not appreciated by every caller who reached them. The machines had, for the most part, not come out of their novelty stage. Now we've gotten used to the answering machine both socially and in business.

For tele-networking, a home answering machine is a must. It's your twenty-four hour secretary. To make it work effectively you have to start with a good receiving message that's readily understandable, and you have to give the caller ample time to leave an adequate message.

Next, and of utmost importance, is your follow-through. Be sure to respond to your messages in a timely manner. If it's used correctly, you should experience little resistance to your answering machine.

Even in the business or professional office the answering machine is becoming more accepted. True, nothing beats being connected to a live voice, but there are occasions when the answering machine is better than nothing.

Typically, we use an answering machine when we close the office for any reason during work hours. It works wonderfully well for those calls that come in after hours or before opening in the morning.

YOUR FAX MACHINE

Sometimes we wish *we* sold fax machines. We believe that the time will come when most homes will have fax equipment just as they have TV sets and washing machines.

Your fax offers the best features of both your telephone and a letter. It's quick, inexpensive and allows you to document information in a printed form. Many of the newer models have other helpful features such as automatic dialing, automatic recall for busy numbers and a built-in answering machine. The writing of this book would have been really tough without the fax to help the two of us to swap notes and to network with those who provided valuable input. We highly recommend fax equipment for all serious networkers.

VOICE MAIL

Voice mail is a form of computer equipment with the ability to receive and store phone messages for many individuals. The effect is that of having a whole series of answering machines for everyone in a company. More and more businesses are going to voice mail to reduce costs and improve efficiency.

Sometimes it's difficult to get used to talking to a voice mail machine, but like the answering machine, you'll soon come to appreciate the voice mailbox when it is properly used.

COMPUTERS

Your personal computer (and we hope you have one) has many capabilities related to tele-networking. With reasonably inexpensive software and a modem, you can maintain your databank, automatically dial anybody in it, have an answering function, have a message leaving function and a memory jogger for call backs.

Though a PC is more expensive than the typical answering machine, the additional capabilities for word processing, accounting, graphics and other features make the investment very profitable.

CELLULAR PHONES

Though previously expensive to own and use, the price of cellular equipment is coming down. We don't advocate cellular phones for everyone, but they do have many advantages, particularly for business people. They do not, however, come without problems.

Cellular phones must be very carefully used in automobiles and require a whole new phone etiquette when they're carried. Just imagine a golfer at a tournament – ready to putt for the championship – and a spectator's cellular phone rings.

HAIL TO THE PHONE

One of your most important networking tools is your telephone, supported by your databank. Used properly, the telephone will help you connect and strengthen the knots in your network.

10

Does Your Business Card Really Mean Business?

How to turn an ordinary card into an "Ace"

It's a ritual that happens millions of times a day, in millions of places – in airports, restaurants, hotels, shops, warehouses and street corners around the world. Two or more business people or professionals meet, talk, and then exchange cards.

For networkers it's almost always the essence of their first contact with a new acquaintance.

How did this universally accepted business custom start? How important is it to networking? Are there etiquette rules for the exchange of cards? Are there ways to make your business card a more effective networking (and sales) tool?

The answers to these questions can make a significant difference in the way you use your business card. It can give you and your business or profession increased visibility, sales and income.

Sometime during the 18th century, English and French aristocrats began exchanging "calling cards." These social cards – about the size of today's business card – were enclosed with gifts, used as mourning cards (given when someone in the family dies), presented when making a social visit, or left behind when no one was at home.

Dr. Walter A. Ostromecki, Jr., an avid business card collector, suggests that the practice of distributing business cards probably grew out of this custom of exchanging one's calling or visiting card. "This was a complimentary gesture of polite society during the 1700's and 1800's," he says. "Socialites who wished their attendance known at gatherings around the community left their cards with their hostess. She, in turn, catalogued them and sent thank-you cards or her own visiting card. She spread the news as to who had attended. It was, in a sense, an early form of networking, as many of the card passers were bankers, attorneys, industrialists, political figures, and so on."

But socialites and social climbers weren't the only ones using calling cards. Darrell L. Christopher, past-president of the United States Business Card Collectors Club, says, "In America in the late 1800's, the rural population used calling cards. The country roads of that era were rough and sometimes treacherous – making it difficult to travel to one's family, neighbors, or friends. Most people worked long hours each day (usually on the farm) and visitors came by infrequently. When a caller arrived and no one was at home, the visitor left a card to show that he had been there. These calling cards came in all sizes and shapes. Many were colorful, filled with flower illustrations and often embossed. The card was printed with the caller's name, and usually carried a brief message such as, 'With my regards.'

"Not much later, a rural merchant decided the sign over his shop did not reach enough people, so he asked a printer to make small, pocket-sized cards listing the shop's business and address. This anonymous entrepreneur's idea turned out to be a winner, for his cards were passed on from customer to customer and even reached different cities.

"A trend was started and continues to this day. These early business cards, engraved or printed from woodcut dies, looked like miniature billboard signs. Some had elaborate ink drawings and most were cluttered with information about the merchant's wares or services."

Contemporary business cards vary in style and usage, according to the character, status or nationality of the giver. In some countries, they're used aggressively to generate business; elsewhere, business people simply use their cards as a means of introduction and later, recall.

WHAT WE CAN LEARN FROM THE JAPANESE

In Japan the exchange of business cards is an extremely important business and social gesture. The exchange of cards, known as *meishi*, occurs after a person has introduced him- or herself and properly bowed. The receiver takes a few moments to read and carefully note the contents of the card, and then returns the bow.

The giver's title affects how he or she will be treated by the receiver. The Japanese attach great importance to titles and companies. Most often the more important the title the more attention and respect is accorded the giver. In some cases, however, junior officers of major companies may be treated with greater respect than senior officers of smaller companies. The ultimate success is to have a business card with no title – it's presumed that you are so well known you don't need one.

Meishi etiquette requires that you always have an ample supply of cards – it's inexcusable to run out. Cards should be carried in an elegant case (distinctive enough to tell something about you), and should be offered with both hands held palm side up – a presentation, not merely an exchange.

In the United States, the exchange of cards runs the gamut from the questionable to the outrageous – from pulling a dog-eared bent, and sometimes dirty card from one's wallet to the antics of Joe Girard, the "world's best car salesman" (according to the Guinness Book of World Records). At sporting events, he often threw hundreds of cards in the air after touchdowns, home runs, and goals. Joe admits that it was a bit unusual, but it did bring him prospects that he turned into car buyers.

There is a middle ground between the very formal cards and their exchange as practiced in the Far East and the advertising business card of the Western world. For professionals and top executives in the West, the more formal and traditional cards – which include the person's name, title or degree, company name and address, and perhaps a corporate logo – are acceptable. In the tradition of the socially conscious Victorians and the Japanese, these cards should be carried in appropriate card cases and presented with an air of dignity. After all, they represent *you.*

Increasingly, small businesses, merchants, and even some professionals are turning to cards that really advertise their business or profession. The trend is definitely toward more creative cards that will attract attention and have long memory retention value.

HOW EFFECTIVE IS YOUR CARD?

The real test of a business card is if the recipient says, "May I keep the card?" Cards that prompt that kind of reply really have to be unique. Fortunately for networkers, with some extra thought, some extra effort, and perhaps, a little extra money, unique cards can be had. They are available through first-class printers or advertising specialty counselors who will be willing to work with you to design something special.

Some of the creative elements that can be tapped are: the material the card is printed on, paper and ink color, type, layout, product or personal photographs and other unique elements of graphic design and texture. The one element that shouldn't be changed is size. Although European and South American cards are sometimes larger than the US standard card (which measures 3.5 inches by 2 inches), it's best to stick to the standard size so the card will fit conveniently into business card cases and filing devices.

Here are a few examples of really creative and unique cards.

A New York City shop called "Clips" distributes a card printed on a see-through plastic bag that holds...yes, different colored paper clips. A direct mail consultant attaches his business card carefully to the front of a book of first class mailing stamps. An Indian lumber broker's card is printed on sandalwood. We know of a rubber manufacturer's card that is printed on rubber sheeting.

A nameplate manufacturer uses a business card sized nameplate. Gerry Ewing, a New Jersey photographer, uses a piece of film carrying his name and information glued to a standard size card. Similarly, a producer of printed circuit cards employs his process to produce his company's cards.

Poland Brothers (a US paper bag and box maker) uses a miniature box for a calling card. The box is collapsible and can be carried flat. Just before the company's sales representative makes a call, the corners of the card are tucked in and a box-shaped business card is presented.

Esko, a Dayton, Ohio manufacturer of custom binders and sales promotional merchandise, has a card shaped and folded to resemble a notebook binder.

Label Art, Inc. takes advantage of its product, peel-off labels, and has created peel-off label business cards that can be filed or stuck on anything.

Trading on the tremendous appeal of Post-It® notes, U-Turn of California, Inc. uses the cover of a pad of sticky notes as its card. C. Perry Conant, manufacturer of steel stamps, uses a narrow chrome-plated steel card.

Business cards have been printed, engraved, or silk screened on almost every imaginable material. They can be embossed or die-cut. Many have drawings of the company's products or photographs of the owners or proprietors. Full-color photo cards are popular and relatively inexpensive.

Have you ever notice how often the recipient of your card turns it over and looks at the back? Some people take advantage of the reverse side of their business cards and include useful information such as calendars, maps, appointment reminders, or a list of products. If you're traveling to Japan, printing a translation in Japanese on the reverse of your card is a must.

HOW MANY CARDS DO YOU GIVE AWAY?

Many business people (and networkers), however do not take full advantage of business cards as advertising or networking tools. When purchasing cards (with a minimum printing usually of 500 pieces) buyers have frequently exclaimed, "What am I going to do with 500 cards? They'll last a lifetime!"

Others never underestimate the power of the business card and can dispose of 500 cards in short order. An executive of a car rental company leaves them with virtually everyone he meets – colleagues at meetings or outings, everyone at a sales call or presentation, his seat partner on planes and trains. (He even leaves his card with a tip at restaurants.)

Once at a beach party, a friend familiar with his habits asked in jest, "Dave, can I have one of your business cards?" You guessed it. Dave handed the startled disbeliever a card from his beach jacket. (Now he plans to carry a supply of cards laminated in plastic to protect them from the sand and water.)

A new trend in the exchange of cards is the use of a Rolodex® file card, the kind with the notches punched at the bottom for insertion in an alphabetically indexed stand. Since these cards exceed the conventional size and their use is limited, they are often given along with a standard business card.

HOW MANY WAYS CAN YOU USE YOUR CARD?

In addition to exchanging cards from hand to hand, other means of distributing cards have come into vogue. Trade groups and even restaurants sponsor "mixers" for business card networking. (More about this in another chapter.)

Space can be rented for the distribution of your cards in wall racks or counter displays at retail locations with high traffic. And don't forget, if you have a business or profession with people coming to you, have a card holder on your desk or counter.

The use of business cards has become so popular in recent years that the concept of the business card format is being used on giveaway products and other specialty advertising items. The business card has been reproduced on such diverse articles as magnets, tape measures, calculators, coasters, and clocks. Cards have also been silk-screened on T-shirts and printed on tote bags.

BUSINESS CARD COLLECTING

Business card collecting has become a hobby for a relatively small but growing number of collectors.

Darrell L. Christopher, a General Motors manager, founded the American Business Card Collectors Club. He founded the club after a co-worker gave him a gift of 800 cards, including some that were quite old. Christopher's 35,000 card collection is divided into some 90 categories.

Other members have even larger collections. Betty Martin of Warsaw, New York, has been accumulating cards since childhood. She has more than 250,000.

Gerald Berg is considered one of the nation's top collectors. His collection of rare and celebrity cards (including one of Adolf Hitler's) is reportedly valued at $250,000. Of course, most business cards have very little monetary value.

To join the 200 members of the American Business Card Club, write the organization in care of: Avery N. Pitzak, President • P.O. Box 460297 • Aurora, CO 80046-0297 • USA

Co-author Ken Erdman would be happy to receive any unusual business cards for his collection. His address: 402 Bethlehem Pike, Philadelphia, PA 19118, USA

TAKE A NEW LOOK AT YOUR BUSINESS CARD

Is it time for you to review your business card habits? Does your card say what it really ought to say or what you want it to say? Does it include your fax number? Is there anything you can put on the back that would be helpful to the receiver? Do you have an ample supply? How about an attractive case to keep your cards presentable?

In short, the big question is: *Does your business card really mean business?*

11

First Class Networking

Sit right down and write someone a letter

One of the most important things we learn in school is how to communicate. It is a skill that is absolutely essential to your success, no matter what career path you follow.

Despite the dramatic innovations in technology – laser beams, fiber optics, memory chips, satellites, etc. – that are changing the way in which we communicate, the written word is still important and will always be.

Letter writing, in particular, continues to be one of the best means there is for communicating with someone, whether for business or personal purposes.

Letters and cards are also the tools of our democracy. They help form opinions and influence our government processes. They also preserve memories and brighten our lives. I can tell you that, personally, there's nothing I look forward to more than a letter from one of my daughters.

Letters and cards will always be a means of both communicating and preserving your thoughts, your feelings, your personality – yourself.

Former Postmaster General
of the United States, William F. Bolger

WHY WRITE?

As we mentioned before, if the average person didn't receive *any* advertising circulars or bills in the daily mail, they probably wouldn't get much mail. (It is estimated that only one out of every eight pieces of mail is a personal letter.) With more reliance on other methods of communication, fewer and fewer personal letters are being written.

Let us remind you that this is good news for networkers. If there is less and less letter writing, then those who do write letters (or send personal mail) command much more attention and appreciation.

Networking letters serve the purpose of keeping in touch with those in your network. The important point is that the letter contact will usually be unexpected, appreciated and long remembered. In spite of the fact that as business people, we get lots of mail, the unexpected personal letter or note from a friend always stands out as something special.

WHEN TO WRITE

The late Thomas B. Constantino, former president of the Noteworthy Company of Amsterdam, New York, scanned newspapers and trade magazines for the names of friends who have made some special contribution to, or achievement in community service. He then sent them a letter to express gratitude and to encourage them to continue their good work. Tom was always pleased at the reaction his letters generated. It was his hope that his small gesture helped motivate those involved to do even more for their community or industry.

In notes from a direct mail seminar at the University of Connecticut presided over by the late, great direct mail expert, Edward Mayer, we found the following additional list of opportunities for *unexpected* good will letters.

1. **Letters of congratulation**
    a. Promotions and new jobs
        - in business
        - in civic organizations

- in social organizations

b. Achievements
   - personal accomplishments (awards, prizes)
   - business accomplishments (records, awards, new products, services)

c. Anniversaries
   - personal birthdays
   - wedding anniversaries
   - company anniversaries
   - service birthdays

d. Acquisitions
   - building a new building
   - starting a new company
   - merger or purchase of an existing company
   - opening of a branch office
   - personal acquisitions, such as a new home

e. Special occasions
   - births
   - marriages
   - graduation
   - recovery from illness

2. Letters of sympathy

a. Death
b. Illness
c. Disaster

3. Letters of welcome

a. Into town (and away from town)
b. Into a community
c. Into an organization
d. Into a customer family
e. To returning military personnel

4. **Thank you letters**
    a. For public service
    b. For personal service
    c. For being a customer
    d. For customer follow-up
    e. For hospitality
    f. For favors or gifts
    g. For special consideration
    h. For compliments

And let's not forget that special discipline of letter writing – part of the Four-mula for Success outlined in Chapter 6 – four letters or notes *every* working day.

TYPES OF LETTERS

Your letters might be as short as one sentence.

There's an old story about a Philadelphia lawyer who wrote a very long letter, in typical legalese, to tell a client's tenant that he must vacate his apartment. The stubborn tenant wasn't about to leave, and he replied to the lengthy letter from the attorney with these few words:

> "Dear Sir:
>
> I remain.
>
> Very truly yours,
> Mr. Sam Jones."

The typical networking letter will probably be no longer than one page. The important part about the networking letter is that it is both personal and informal. Handwritten messages work the best, but typed letters are far better than no letters.

OTHER WAYS TO USE THE MAIL

In addition to the letter there are other opportunities to use the mail to stay in touch with those in your network or those you want to get into your network. You can also use the mail to send clippings, articles from magazines, or photos along with a short note. This concept is a short-cut to letter writing but it is equally appreciated. Often networkers devise a personalized enclosure or use a stock cartoon enclosure to send with the articles and on which to write a short note.

Once you get known for sending items of interest to friends and acquaintances, you'll be surprised at how many of the recipients start returning the favor.

PHOTOS ARE SPECIAL

There is something magical about photographs. How often have you had your picture taken but have never seen the results? For most of us it's a frequent experience. Here again is a great opportunity to capitalize on fulfilling a desire – that of seeing oneself in a photograph. Think about it. How often do you throw away photographs? Many people we know don't even throw away those out-of-focus ones or photos with body parts cut off. How nice it is to receive a photo or two included in a letter or greeting card!

BUCK SLIPS, NOTES AND MEMOS

Other alternatives to the letter are buck slips, notes and memos. These differ from letters in that they are smaller and usually on note-sized paper. Frequently the sender designs his or her own personalized note paper. Instead of "From the desk of:" stationery, use distinctive note or letter paper that can be identified immediately as coming from you. Use colored paper, a cartoon, a logo, or even a particular style of pen to individualize your notes.

GREETING CARDS ARE GREAT

Most people are used to receiving greeting cards for Valentine's Day, birthdays, Christmas and Hanukkah. How about other occasions and holidays? Let's not forget the possibilities of Thanksgiving, Independence Day, St. Patrick's day, the first day of Spring, even Bastille Day. In fact, there's a special reason to celebrate for every day of the year. Most libraries have ***Chase's Annual Events***, a book which lists events, observances, anniversaries, birthdays and celebrations throughout the year. It might not be easy to find greeting cards for some of these celebrations, but blank greeting cards are available with a wide variety of designs. If you really want to be creative you can design your own card from stock paste up art and your photo copier; or you can use your computer and its graphic capabilities to design cards. The surprise of a greeting card at an unexpected time it not soon forgotten.

GETTING STARTED WITH YOUR LETTERS

Not unlike professionals writers, most people have a little trouble getting their letters started. Once started, however the rest of the letter seems to flow rather easily. The following self-starters, also from direct mail authority Ed Mayer, should be useful.

Letter Self-Starters

1. **To say "Thank You"**
   - Thank you for taking the time and trouble to write as you did.
   - We were really pleased to receive your order.
   - I really enjoyed visiting with you at...
   - It was so nice of you to...
   - Thank you for being so courteous to our sales person when he/she was in to see you last week.
   - Welcome to the family!
   - It was a real treat to...
   - I liked your letter. It was heart-warming to read it and know that...

2. **To convey good news**
   - I have some good news for you.
   - It is a real pleasure to say that...
   - I know you'll be glad to hear that...
   - I thought you might like to see the enclosed.

- You will be hearing a lot about...
- I am glad to say that we can help you.
- You will be glad to know that...
- This is an important announcement about...
- This letter brings you good news.

3. **To make an explanation**
    - I think what happened is this.
    - We have now had a chance to...
    - As you probably know...
    - It may sound strange to say this...
    - You'll be glad to know that everything is all right with...

4. **To ask a favor**
    - I wonder is you would mind doing me a favor?
    - Will you lend us a helping hand?
    - I wonder if it would be possible...
    - Will you do me a great favor?
    - Will you please...
    - I wonder if you would mind helping us out of a little difficulty.
    - Within the next few days could you...

(See Chapter 18, *The Nine Magic Words of Networking,* for more discussion on asking for help.)

5. **To extend an invitation**
    - You are most cordially invited to...
    - It will be a real privilege to...
    - Would you like to come to...
    - Will you be our guest at...

6. **To express regret or offer an apology**
    - I only wish it were possible...
    - I certainly agree with you that...
    - Is my face red!

- I know I would feel the same way myself if...
- If you ever saw a person behind the 8-ball...
- What happened to you just shouldn't happen to anyone.
- I wish I could tell you in person how sorry we are that...
- I am sorry we didn't make it clear...
- Much as we would like to...
- I wish I could be with you at your meeting.
- Thank you for your invitation. I'm flattered and wish that...

7. **To offer congratulations**
   - You are certainly to be congratulated.
   - It was very nice to hear that...
   - I have read with great interest about...
   - You are certainly on the right track.
   - Congratulations – from all of us here at...on your...
   - I thought you did an outstanding job as...

8. **Miscellaneous unclassified**
   - Someone once said...
   - One day last week...
   - I just came back from lunch with...
   - This afternoon I saw the advance plans for...
   - Yes, I'll be glad to...

LETTER WRITING TIPS

We assume that everybody knows how to write a letter. But like most assumptions, this might not always be true. We can assume, however, that not everybody can write a really good letter.

Here are some guidelines to help make your letters easier to read and more interesting.

1) Plan your letter. Think about what you want to say and get your thoughts in logical sequence. If you are going to use to same letter to more than one person in your network, a written outline of what you want to say will be helpful.

2) Use short words, short sentences and short paragraphs. In his book ***Direct Marketing: How You Can Really Do It Right,*** author Ray Jutkins suggests that for every 100 words you write, double-check to make sure 70 of those words are 5 letters or less. Sentences should be short. Only one idea to a sentence. Keep sentences to an average of 14 words, 25 syllables.

Paragraphs should be short, with no more than seven lines of copy before you break for a new one. There is no rule that says the same thought can't carry over into two or three more paragraphs, just limit paragraphs to seven lines.

3) Write in a conversational style. Don't use stilted phrases. Picture the reader(s) in your mind as you write.

4) Avoid words that might not be readily understood.

5) Where possible, use the active voice rather than the passive voice. It makes your letters sparkle.

6) Avoid overuse of the word *that*.

7) Watch out for too many personal pronouns. People want to hear what's important to *them,* not what's important to *you.*

8) Where possible use colorful words. H. Phelps Gates told readers of the ***Christian Science Monitor*** about the effect of words on readers. He listed the strength and force in short words: blast, boom, throb, thump, clank, chime, hiss and buzz. He then mentioned words you can "hear" like the *swish* of silk, and words that convey a sense of smell like *musk* and *cheese* and *mint* and *rose.*

9) Look for opportunities to substitute verbs for nouns. This will give greater clarity and force to your writing.

10) Edit your letters. Reread them carefully to make sure you have said what you wanted to say. Your letter should be friendly and easy to read. Check your spelling and punctuation.

LETTERS: THE WRIGHT THING TO DO

An article in the ***Honolulu Star Bulletin*** by Mike Gordon described a unique letter writing project sponsored by Rod Wright from the Marketing Department of the United States Postal Service, Honolulu Field Division.

Wright devised his letter writing campaign when he realized that all the postal service had planned to do to promote its services before the Christmas crunch was to designate October as stamp collecting month.

To promote *his* cause, letter writing, Wright got the postal service and the Department of Education to sponsor a statewide contest in letter writing among students in grades one through twelve.

The initial response from students was so great that Wright added a division for adults in secondary education classes.

Winners were invited (by letter, naturally) to an award ceremony at the state capital.

"We'd hoped to call attention to letter writing and have people understand that letters are appreciated," says Wright. "Even though it takes a little trouble to write a letter, the person who receives it really feels what you're feeling."

Wright has proof that letters last. He has letters that were written by his grandmother 28 years ago. They're among his most prized possessions, a free ticket to the past. "And letters," says Wright with all the zeal of a preacher, "don't have to be long."

Start today. Sit right down and write someone a letter.

12

You're Bigger News Than You Think

Public relations networking

PUBLIC RELATIONS

He who whistles
down a well,

About the goods
he has to sell,

Will never glean
the golden dollars,

As he who scales the heights
and hollers.

Press releases and your local media may be networking's best kept secrets. They're inexpensive (you don't have to pay for space) and they're more believable than paid advertising. They are effective in situations where paid advertising isn't appropriate.

PUBLIC RELATIONS IN THE NETWORKING MIX

Networking is one of the places where paid advertising might not be appropriate but where public relations will fill the need.

Typical examples for publicity might include announcements of: job promotions, changes of address, honors and awards earned, books written, new accounts gained, speaking engagements...and the list goes on.

The advantage of public relations as a networking tool is that it provides an opportunity to get your message to a wide audience quickly and inexpensively. Your news also brings acquaintances up-to-date with what is happening to you. It also allows people who are not already in your network to learn about you and the positive things you are doing.

There was a picture and caption in the ***Ocean City Sentinel Ledger*** newspaper showing the city publicist wearing a batting helmet with a megaphone device mounted on its top. From the cap there was a wire to a kazoo. The caption explained that the unit was an electric kazoo, the brain child of Mark Fox and would be used in an upcoming Do-Da (crazy costume) parade.

Ken Erdman noticed the story and thought to himself, "I've just got to get one of those electric kazoos for my friend Wally 'Famous' Amos." Wally is famous for playing kazoos as well as for his chocolate chip cookies. Ken called the newspaper in New Jersey and found that the inventor lived only minutes away from him in Pennsylvania. A call to Mark Fox resulted in a luncheon, an electric kazoo and a small consulting job for Ken.

But the story doesn't end here. Ken had invited Wally to speak on the subject of illiteracy at a convention in Oregon. (Wally Amos is the National Spokesperson for Literacy.) Prior to Wally's speaking, Ken gave him the kazoo hat. A Portland news photographer spotted Wally in the electric kazoo hat and snapped a picture – which appeared in the next day's paper! More publicity for Mark Fox.

And still the story doesn't end. Ken sent a note to the gossip column editor at Wally's hometown newspaper in Honolulu mentioning the gift of the world's first electric kazoo. The columnist used the item – then he wrote another item about the name of Ken's company, The Three Marketeers, Inc., mentioning the originality of the name.

Here was P.R. networking starting on the shores of the Atlantic and getting all the way to the furthest United States shore on the Pacific.

GOOD LUCK?

Was the success of the kazoo story just a matter of good luck? Perhaps. But more likely it was the product of disciplined public relations networking. Somebody had to recognize the opportunities – and then act upon them.

The element of luck is always present in public relations but knowing how to recognize news and how to present it to the right medium reduces the luck factor. We believe that the important things in your life are often bigger news than you think they are. We also believe that most people have a better than average chance of having their news published or broadcasted than they think they have. Especially when the news is presented to the media properly.

PITY THE POOR EDITOR

How do you properly present the news to the media? Let's talk about press releases to newspapers and magazines first.

There is a prescribed form for sending news to editors. Why must you use the prescribed form? Editors receive press releases in every kind of way imaginable. Some come scribbled on tablet paper. Some arrive daintily handwritten on pastel-colored, perfumed note paper and some even come written on the backs of envelopes as notes taken during a meeting.

Part of an editor's job is to read press releases and look for suitable news. Remember, a newspaper is made up of news from wire services, information from its own reporters, editorial material...and the news from press releases. Editors *need* your news. Unfortunately, if they have to decipher handwriting, find their noses tickled by perfume, or are forced to cope with unmanageable paper, your chances for getting your material read are slim to none. Let's not tax the eyesight or patience of the very people we want to help us.

WINNING THE BATTLE OF THE WASTEBASKET

To get your press release used, you first have to win the "Battle of the Wastebasket." Editors go through many, many releases for each issue. If the releases are not really news, or if they're hard to read or understand they go into the wastebasket. Your job is to keep your release out of the trash.

Follow these guidelines, and we'll guarantee that your press release will have a *better than average* chance of being used.

1. Make sure that what you send is really newsworthy. If it's not, or if you continually send unimportant news, you'll be like the boy who cried wolf. Your really important news will be overlooked.

2. Type your release on plain white 8.5" X 11" paper.

3. Have a name and address block for the sender at the top of the release.

4. Mark the release in large type: "PRESS RELEASE" or "NEWS RELEASE" or just plain "NEWS."

5. Under the heading, "For Further Information" add the name and phone number of someone who can officially and intelligently answer questions concerning the release.

6. Provide a date line for the release telling when the news can be released. This might be the date the release is sent or a later date. If, for instance, your release tells about something someone is expected to say on a future date, make sure the release is marked: "For Release After (applicable date)." This way, if something happens to the speaker or they don't actu-

ally say what the release says they will, you still have time to retract the news.

8. Double space your release (so editors can write between the lines).

9. Leave wide margins on both sides (again, so editors have a place to write).

10. Title your release with a headline that very briefly tells what the release is about.

11. Your first sentence must relate the pertinent facts. Answer the Kipling quotation: "I have five servants, tried and true. Their names are what and when and where and why and who."

12. The paragraphs following should contain the details of the story. Remember to use short words, short sentences and short paragraphs.

13. In these succeeding paragraphs present your news in descending order with the most important information first and the least important last. Editors edit to size from the bottom up. If they have to cut your news, let them cut the least important information.

14. If your material runs to more than one page mark the bottom of your release: "– more –." On the following page repeat the headline in case the two pages get separated. Please do not staple pages. Be kind to the editor.

At the end of the release use the symbols "– 30 –" or "###" in the center of the page. This tells the editor there is no more to the release.

HOW TO HANDLE PHOTOGRAPHS

If you include photographs, these suggestions will help:

1. Editors prefer black and white photos. In a pinch, a good color print will work.

2. Size should be at least 4" X 5", although 8" X 10" is often preferred. Again, in a pinch you may get away with a smaller size, but remember you lessen your chances of winning "the battle of the wastebasket."

3. Try to use some creativity in taking the picture. Look for the special interest angle. Avoid the two people passing a check between them. Watch your backgrounds (no flag poles coming out of the tops of heads).

4. Be sure to accurately identify everyone in the picture.

5. Attach a caption under the photo that includes the names of the people in the picture. This is then pasted to the back of the picture with the type showing under it.

6. Crop the photo to the tightest possible shot leaving out extraneous background.

7. Do not clip the photo to the release with a paper clip. This might leave a mark that will cause damage to the print.

8. Mail the picture with some kind of firm backing to make sure it doesn't crack or bend.

WHERE TO SEND YOUR PRESS RELEASES

Now that you've finished your release you can mail it to the editor of the appropriate publication. To increase your chances of having your news in print, you might specifically address your release to the editor most likely to use it. Your choices might include the entertainment editor, the business editor, the society editor, the travel editor, the sports editor, the fashion editor or the food editor.

RADIO AND TV NETWORKING

Yes, there are opportunities to network through radio and TV. The likelihood of getting mentioned on the regular radio news segments is less than appearing in the press. There is still the opportunity, however, for public service announcements (PSA's), the community bulletin board or for interviews on talk shows.

A PSA is a short release (usually from 10 to 30 seconds) scripted for radio or TV and usually for a non-profit organization. It may be general in nature (promoting a cause), or specific, perhaps announcing an upcoming event.

The style of the PSA is much like that of a press release except that you use a "kill date" – the PSA will play up until that date. If there is not a specific time limit, you can make a note to that effect.

TALK SHOWS

If you are an expert on a particular subject, approach your local stations for the opportunity to appear on a talk show. Just as the press needs news to fill space, stations need input to fill time.

CABLE TV

Though regular TV news coverage is the toughest to get (though not impossible), cable TV is a good source for "newsy" subjects. People profiles, news of trade shows, conventions, seminars, unusual occupations, travelers, experts on timely subjects, etc. are all potential material for cable. Call the station and give them your concept.

ARTICLES FOR THE MEDIA

You do not have to be a professional writer (only a good writer) to develop articles on your favorite subject for newspapers, magazines, trade journals or newsletters. The articles can be short or long. If they're too long they will be shortened by the editor.

CAPITALIZING ON WHAT'S BEEN PUBLISHED

Having gotten some press coverage, you have a wonderful opportunity to further your networking process. Send reprints of the items published by or about you to others in your network who might be interested. Some of the better networkers we know who use newsletters often include their published news with them.

A reverse procedure is also an effective networking concept. When you read about someone in your network, clip the article and mail it to that person with a short note of congratulations.

PUBLIC RELATIONS NETWORKING

Public relations efforts include more than the traditional media exposure for you news. Other facets of the medium include such areas as celebrations, special events, public speaking, articles, newsletters, etc.

For more detailed information on public relations, see the reading list in the Toolbox Section.

13

Your Network Newsletter

Homemade news

In addition to getting your name in the press through other concerted public relations efforts, you can create a newsletter – your own media – for your personal news.

A communications concept that grew up in the '80's as a paid circulation vehicle, newsletters have matured and are even more popular in the '90's – both as paid and unpaid subscriptions.

It's estimated that there are approximately 2,000 commercial paid subscription newsletters, covering virtually every subject imaginable. We recently read of a newsletter devoted to people interested in eating insects. ***The Food Insects Newsletter***, with a circulation of 600, was founded by Dr. R. DeFoliart, an entomologist at the University of Wisconsin.

The popularity and success of newsletters is based on quick, personal news of specific interest to the reader. Newsletters also tend to get completely read rather than skimmed. Unlike magazines, newsletters frequently don't carry advertising. They're shorter than magazines, yet they provide information and news in an easy-to-read form. Because they don't offer advertising, paid subscription newsletters can be very expensive, based upon the kind of news or highly specialized information they provide. Investment or forecasting newsletters fit into this category. The subscription costs have given newsletters built-in credibility and high perceived value. Free subscription newsletters have benefited from the reputation of the paid subscription letters.

For the purposes of networking, this chapter is about free newsletters – the kind you will probably produce yourself and mail to those people in your personal network.

ARE NEWSLETTERS REALLY APPRECIATED?

David Ogilvy, the great advertising genius, says, "Editorial material is three times more persuasive than advertising. While Americans have developed negative attitudes toward most advertising, they've developed positive attitudes toward informative advertising."

How many conversations are started with a combination of words that basically ask: "What's new?" Most. People are preoccupied with "what's new." Therefore the *news* in newsletters is always appreciated and gains readership.

Newsletter news is not the dramatic news of the papers but rather news within the circles of influence of the reader. People like to be "in on things."

UNIVERSITY OF MARYLAND STUDY

The University of Maryland conducted a study to determine what motivated employees. They asked two groups, employees and employers to place, in order of importance, factors that impacted upon job performance. These included: work appreciation, being "in on things," employer sympathy for personal problems, job security, wages, interesting work, promotions, employer loyalty, good working conditions and tactful discipline.

The employees listed being "in on things" as their #2 most important performance motivator. (Appreciation was #l and salary was surprisingly #5.) If employees feel this strongly about being "in on things," a newsletter must rank high as a communications (internal network) tool.

THE NEWSLETTER AS A NETWORKING TOOL

Because newsletters can be easy to read and contain information that people usually want to read, they are ideal for networking. They are easy to put together and distribute. You have control over the material they contain. They are relatively inexpensive. A news format has a high degree of believability. You can use a newsletter for your business, corporate charitable or personal use.

In her book ***Marketing With Newsletters,*** author Elaine Floyd, suggests that newsletters work particularly well for:

- bringing in supporters
- selling more to existing customers
- improving morale
- informing and educating
- increasing involvement
- attracting volunteers
- bringing back lost customers
- winning support
- boosting donations
- unifying a community of readers.

Ms. Floyd further suggests, "In order to achieve these goals, however, newsletters have to be read. The newsletters people read contain useful information presented in appropriate and appealing ways.

"Successful promotional newsletters get people to read not only what interests them, but also what the publisher want them to read."

Your audience is the key for gaining the most networking value from your newsletter. There are basically two kinds of audiences: your internal audience or in-house newsletter (for employees, members, etc.) and your external audience for the other people in your network.

SELF-PUBLISHED NEWSLETTERS

The newsletters of most interest to networkers are the self-published newsletters. They can be published by your business, profession, charity, civic or service club – or they can be published by an individual.

Newsletters need not be published on a regular basis. In fact, in some instances it's better not to promise a regular schedule because it puts you under a deadline (and we all know the potential danger of deadlines).

Newsletters vary widely in layout. Some are done in columns and some are done with type going completely across the page. Some contain photographs or are lavishly illustrated and some have no illustrations or photos.

The most familiar and accepted newsletter format seems to be the 8.5″ X 11″ four page newsletter. The audiences and content will vary in size depending upon who is publishing.

GETTING STARTED WITH A NEWSLETTER

Your first consideration is a name for your newsletter and possibly a logo (you could include the logo of your business or you might want a separate one just for the newsletter). Next you'll incorporate the name and logo into a masthead that contains the pertinent publishing information.

At this stage you might want to incorporate some color into the design of the masthead. To save money, if you do use color in your masthead, you can have "shells" printed – paper with only the masthead done in color. You then print these shells as you need them with only the cost of black and white type (printed by your local printer, with your computer or on your photo copier).

The next consideration is the type format. Do you use columns or go straight across the page? Do you use typewriter type or do you have type set? For a not-so-fancy, but completely acceptable newsletter you can type across your sheet. Remember, however to use short words, short sentences and short paragraphs. Make it easy to read. We also recommend headlines or sub-heads to preview each news item.

If you have computer capabilities you can get involved in desk-top publishing – adding graphics, columns and other formats.

WHAT'S NEWS?

Having decided on how to put your newsletter together, the next decision is content. Remember it's a *news*letter so the content should be timely. The news should be of *real* interest to your audience. In addition to news you can provide helpful information.

Again, turning to ***Marketing With Newsletters,*** Elaine Floyd suggests, "When choosing your newsletter's content, first look at the hard news you have for supporters and prospects – new services, special events and so on. Then search for information that keeps readers involved and interested in your subject – how to's, other people's products, worksheets, calendars, etc. These increase your newsletter's value and keeps prospects reading time after time."

News for your personal networking newsletter can include:

- What's happened to you since your last newsletter (travels, special events, accomplishments, speeches, articles published, etc.).

- A calendar of your future travels, including details, which you'll update with each newsletter.

- A specific report on your work – new projects, clients customers, etc. since your last newsletter.

- Helpful information for the readers which you may have collected from many sources.

• Projects or work you are interested in taking on in the future.

Your newsletter can be designed to provide a space for address and postage when folded. The letter then works as a self-mailer, eliminating the cost of an envelope.

THE "HAMMER" IN YOUR NETWORKING TOOLBOX

As a serious networker you should consider producing a newsletter to reach your various networks. Your newsletter might be a simple as a "one pager" written for your family and friends, or as extensive as a multi-page effort for your business, profession or association. It might be published as often as weekly or as seldom as "once-in-a-while." The important thing is that you do it. Newsletters are the "hammer" in your networking toolbox.

"The World's Smallest Newsletter," printed on a standard 4" X 6" postcard.

imp

The World's Smallest Newsletter

Published every now and then by:

BOB WESTENBERG

Copywriter / Consultant / Fund Raiser

6020-E Highway 179 • Sedona, AZ 86336 • (602) 284-1111

Who eats out most often in U.S.? Men 18 to 24; 50-64 year-olds; college graduates; Southerners; city-dwellers.

Study shows business / industrial ads can be repeated four times without losing their effectiveness.

Religions / denominations that come closest to tithing: Jews 3.8% of household income; Baptists 2.3%; Presbyterians 2.1%; Catholics 1.3%. (Per *Investment Vision.)*

Check your next sales letter. Cover up first two paragraphs, often unnecessary. Letters may be improved by deleting them.

If you have to stay awake longer than usual, 15 minute naps every 4 hours better than no sleep at all. You perform better. Leonardo da Vinci did this.

Sign in cocktail lounge in Norway: "Ladies are requested not to have children in the bar, please."

Senior job-hunting executives can expect to spend average nine months finding a new job. Number of high ticket (6-figure) positions is shrinking.

Only about half of car owners have work done on free auto recall repairs.

Average monthly house payment (principal, interest, tax, insurance) for first-time home buyers: $1,154 in Northeast; $1,126 in West; $812 in Midwest; $711 in the South.

A ride on the Moscow subway (world's cheapest) is a penny. London is most expensive - $1.17.

Letter / circular / action piece in a direct mailing will almost always pull better than a self-mailer.

Stress-fighting thought: 100 years from now, who is going to care if you were stuck in traffic?

Phone tip: Try to be the last one to hang up in case caller thinks of something else to say. Also better for him to hear your voice last instead of "the click."

Break only one bad habit at a time. Do it when not pressured; set realistic goals. Don't get discouraged if not on schedule. Reward yourself regularly.

To reach the boss personally, try phoning about 8:45 a.m. (his time). Some get in before their secretaries.

To all of you who are clients, thank you for your business. To all of you who are friends, thank your for your friendship. To all IMP readers, a happy, stress-free, fulfilling holiday time.

14

Specialize Your Network

With imprinted advertising specialties

What are advertising specialties?

Good question.

Many people, particularly those who have not used specialties, might not recognize them by their correct name. The imprinted promotional products industry has a minor identity problem.

Specialties have been called premiums, souvenirs, give-aways, and even advertising gimmicks.

An advertising specialty is correctly defined as a product that is usually inexpensive and useful. It carries an advertiser's identity (address, phone, etc.), logo or sales message and it's given freely...no strings attached.

Premiums – often confused with specialties – differ from specialties because they are normally more expensive and they are usually given with strings attached. Normally you have to do or buy something to receive a premium.

WHY NETWORK WITH ADVERTISING SPECIALTIES?

Because advertising specialties are inexpensive, useful, come with the giver's identification, and are given as gifts, they are ideal networking tools.

People love to receive things. A gift, no matter how small and inconsequential it may seem to the giver, is very important to the recipient...it means something special to them. By giving a specialty item imprinted with company or personal identification, you've reinforced your message beyond the business card. (Sometimes a specialty can serve as a business card. See Chapter 10, *Does Your Business Card Really Mean Business*, to learn how to combine the best elements of both business cards and specialties.)

Specialty advertising as a form of networking has a time release impact. A message read or heard only once is 66% forgotten within 24 hours and is practically out of mind in 30 days. A message that is read or heard several times a day for 8 days is virtually memorized. At the end of 30 days, the memory retains 90% of the message. An inexpensive imprinted advertising specialty allows you to get your networking message in front of your audience and keep it there as they use their gift over and over again.

With careful selection, life expectancy of an advertising specialty and its message far exceeds that of any other medium. Although imprinted promotional products are described using the word "advertising," they are used for purposes other than pure advertising. Advertising specialties are widely employed in a corporation's marketing mix as incentives, awards and for recognition. Specialties are also used for public relations, politics and community relations.

THE O'HARE POLL

DOWNTIME Broadcasting Company, a specialty advertising audio tape communications group, reports that in a poll of 146 people conducted at O'Hare International Airport in Chicago, 63% of those interviewed stated that they were either carrying or wearing an imprinted specialty item. Forty two percent of that group stated that they had the item for at least six months. But the most important statistic of all was that more than three quarters of these people were able to recall the name or message prior to revealing the specialty to the pollster.

Do people really appreciate inexpensive *free* gifts with someone's name or advertising message?

You bet they do!

We're reminded of the story of a foursome of bankers playing golf at an elite country club. One of the golfers hit his ball into a clear, shallow pond. When he went to retrieve the ball, using one of his clubs to reach it, he noticed that there were several other balls just beyond his. In an effort to get a couple of free balls, he overextended himself and wound up with both feet in the water and mud of the pond. His golf shoes were a mess. The moral of the story is that the golfer could well afford golf balls, but he still sacrificed an extremely expensive pair of golf shoes to get the *free* balls.

And if you're still not convinced of how much people appreciate – and use – imprinted promotional products, try the O'Hare poll. Ask people in your network if they have any imprinted items in their pocket, purse, automobile, or desk.

You'll be hard-pressed to find someone who answers no.

HOW TO NETWORK WITH ADVERTISING SPECIALTIES

Since a major attribute of imprinted advertising products is memory retention, they are particularly useful for your first meeting with someone, either in person or by mail. They can also be used as thank you gifts for favors. Many networkers give specialties to receptionists or secretaries. They can be used as hand-outs at trade shows. As speakers and seminar leaders we often provide imprinted writing instruments and pads for attendees. Specialties can be given at the close of a sale as appreciation gifts. Real estate people often give specialties at the closing of house sales. A friend of ours who runs a catering service presents his clients with the pen they have used to sign their contract.

WALKING BILLBOARDS

Almost everybody wears some form of imprinted clothing.

In the specialty industry the clothing is know as wearables. Wearables include: hats and caps, T-shirts, shirts, ties, sweat shirts, belts, sport shorts, socks, shoes and just about anything else you can think of to wear.

In the retail trade, fashion conscious people buy designer logo clothes – also referred to as signature clothes – at premium prices. There was a time when we hid labels. Now it's trendy to show off the manufacturer's name or logo.

Imagine the networking impact of someone wearing something for all to see that has *your* name, message or logo on it.

Not only are people willing to wear something with an advertising (networking) message, but more importantly they seem to do it with a certain sense of pride. When you wear a cap or jacket from your school, fire company, employer, or service club, you're really networking for that group.

SELECTING A SPECIALTY

There are thousands of specialties from which to chose. A good starting point for the selection of a specialty for your networking purposes should be your budget. How much can you spend and how many pieces will you need? Another consideration is how you are going to distribute your specialties. If you are going to mail them, you have to add in the postage cost. Next, you should consider how appropriate your specialty is to your personality, your business or profession and your audience. A beverage distributor might give bottle and can openers. An automobile dealer could give an emergency flashlight, tire gauge or road atlas. A real estate broker could provide an imprinted yard stick or tape measure for the new buyer to use to measure space for furniture.

Carol Walker of Spartan Promotional Group, Inc. of St. Paul, Minnesota (and who helped immensely with this chapter) told us about some of the specialties she uses: "Personally I have had lots of fun giving away inexpensive items with my name on them. Lately, I've been using a magnet in the shape of an arrow with the tagline, 'For new directions in advertising, call...' Whoever I give it to immediately puts it on a file cabinet or on their desk where they see it many times a day – it's like having my business card always right in front of their eyes.

"When I call on corporate executives who have wood furniture I give them a plastic coaster with my advertising imprint. Usually they will use it right away for their coffee cup – again, my 'business card' is in front of them where they will see it every day."

Don Craighead, to whom Tom has dedicated this book, hands out a "Golden Attitude" pin, to be worn on the lapel of your suit or dress. It reminds you to always maintain a golden (positive) attitude. The pin also elicits questions from others and is a great networking icebreaker.

Promotional products are often used to create a special effect or to dramatize an important moment. Imprinted flashlights have been distributed to audiences who will turn them on in a darkened room to tie in with the speaker's message. Balloon drops are a popular way to dramatize an important event. Of course, the items were imprinted with a logo or message as reminder advertising.

WHERE TO BUY SPECIALTIES

Advertising specialties are produced by thousands of manufacturers and are sold through three primary sources. Most specialties are sold through advertising specialty distributors, whose salespeople are known as counselors. Some are sold through what are known in the specialty industry as direct houses, and some are sold by mail order.

ADVERTISING SPECIALTY DISTRIBUTORS

Advertising specialty distributors are your local sources for specialties. They are often small business people working in the immediate area of their offices, but can also be multi-million dollar corporations serving the entire nation. Counselors should be well trained to not only provide products but to also help you with concept and product ideas. They will also help you pick products within your budget, suggest distribution methods and research specialties that will particularly fit you audience. Several advantages of local advertising specialty distributors are the convenience of a local office, showrooms maintained by many distributors where you can see samples of products, and the close personal contact with a nearby source.

DIRECT HOUSES

Direct houses usually provide national coverage by a team of company-employed salespeople reporting to a national headquarters. Ordering from a direct house doesn't mean that you will get discount prices because you are buying "direct." Rather, the direct house is a form of distribution using company controlled and trained salespeople in a wide geographical area.

MAIL ORDER SOURCES

The third possibility for buying specialties is by mail order – from the catalogs you receive at the office or your home.

Sometimes the mail order catalogs are perceived as offering lower prices than those from direct houses or distributors. Studies have shown, however, that this is not usually true. Catalog pricing tends to match that of local distributors. The catalogs may also offer free gifts with your order or some other "special offer" device to get you to order.

Though the prices may be advertised as very low, or the free goods very enticing, you sacrifice the personal attention and ideas available from other sources.

Sources for imprinted promotional items are listed in the classified section of your phone book under the heading "Advertising Specialties."

WHEN TO BUY SPECIALTIES

Every networker should have a least one specialty to give away to remind people of who you are and what you do. In addition to this specialty, there are many occasions when you should use additional specialties for specific purposes. To name just a few: if you move, get promoted, change your phone number, throw a party, take an exciting vacation, run a seminar, celebrate holidays or weddings.

Weddings? Really? Yes!

Beth Bauer, who runs a Philadelphia based advertising specialty distributorship, provided guests at her wedding reception with after-dinner chocolates imprinted with the names of the bride and groom and the date of the wedding.

HOW TO BUY SPECIALTIES

Just as there are "discount" sources for most products, there are those who will always be ready to "offer you a little something off" catalog or list prices. You should recognize that in many instances you will be sacrificing something. Usually that something is composed of quality, on-time delivery, research and service. Advertising specialty pricing is based on providing a fair margin to the supplier who supplies the four very important elements mentioned. Stories abound of people who bought a little cheaper but received their specialties with misspelled words, in wrong colors or too late.

Another consideration for the buyer is "shopping" creative product ideas developed for your particular program. If a counselor creates a unique program for you with recommended products, it's really not fair to then look for the lowest prices from someone who didn't provide the creative aspects of your program. Creative talent should be recognized as part of the catalog pricing. Anybody can sell a commodity – creative ideas are a lot harder to come by. Your best possible source for specialties is the one that can come up with really great ideas and provide the research to find just the right product.

TRADE SHOWS, SEMINARS AND THE OPEN HOUSE

Advertising specialty trade associations often run trade shows for local customers and prospects. Manufacturers sometimes provide seminars, in co-operation with trade associations, to offer educational opportunities for the trade. Distributors with show rooms will, from time to time, host an open house for clients and prospects. These are all excellent opportunities to learn more about imprinted advertising specialties and how to use them to both support and enlarge your networks.

Ad specialties are inexpensive, long remembered and always appreciated. Give the people in your network something to think about: give them an imprinted advertising specialty carrying your name and information.

15

Shhhhhhhhh!

Listen for success

Successful networking is based upon effective communications. According to Dr. Lyman K. Steil, Executive Director of the International Listening Association, we communicate about 80% of our working time. Writing accounts for only about 9% of that time. Reading accounts for 16%. Speaking accounts for 30%, and listening accounts for 45% of our communications time.

Communication is obviously a two-way process. You write, someone reads. Someone speaks, you listen.

Is this always true? No, not always. Or at least not effectively.

In school all of us had extensive training in reading and writing. But what about listening? Listening is a skill just like reading and writing. From the above figures, listening would seem even more important than reading or writing, and yet for the most part, we get no specific training in listening.

LEARNING ABOUT LISTENING

Perhaps thousands of books have been written on the subjects of salesmanship and public speaking, all telling how to better present ourselves verbally and how to get our message across. But there's a dearth of books on listening, the connecting communications link. If there is a "listening" message in any of these sales books, it is that salespeople run the risk of talking too much and not listening enough or carefully enough. They tend to spend too much time talking about what they have to sell and not enough time listening to what the customer wants.

At one time or another we've all been guilty of not listening carefully enough to the message being presented.

Remember the game "Pass It On" we played as youngsters? You whispered a message to the person sitting next to you, and then he whispered it to the person next to him, who whispered it on to the person next to her, and so on, and so on. At the end of the line, the resulting message was not at all like the original one. That's one of the possible results of a lack of careful listening.

And then there's the issue of "polite" listening. This is where we appear attentive to seem courteous, but we don't really listen to the message. There's an old story that best illustrates this failing in listening traits. It's about two people who meet during a cocktail party. "How are things?" the first fellow asks. "Not good," was the reply. "My wife is in the hospital with cancer, my son was caught using drugs and my thirteen year old daughter is pregnant." "Glad to hear it! Pass on my regards," came the reply. "Polite" listening!

Still another problem is not taking time to listen. We want to hurry up the slow speaker or the "wordy" speaker. We might interrupt or finish the speaker's sentence. Our message here is, hurry up, we don't have time to or want to listen. And there is the subject of eye contact. Perhaps we don't look the speaker in the eye during a conversation or we're easily distracted. That presents the opportunity for missing the message.

And finally, in this short discourse on effective listening, there is the problem of talking so much that little or no time is left to listen. People who do this are often considered bores, yet talking too much is a common habit.

NETWORKING LISTENERS

Successful networkers know how to use listening as the powerful tool it is. Networkers can adopt good listening habits that will substantially increase both what they can learn through verbal networking and the kind of image they present to those with whom they network.

Perhaps the best place to start an effort to improve our listening skills is to learn what other people consider annoying listening habits. See the end of this chapter for a list of thirty annoying listening habits presented by Pat Payer, seminar leader of Florida, and Dr. Stephen Boyd at a listening seminar sponsored by the Specialty Advertising Association International.

To become a more effective listener, take the steps necessary to overcome these annoying habits. Additionally, follow the Boy Scout motto: Be Prepared. Before attending a mixer or making a networking phone call, say to yourself, "I'm going to actively listen." For face-to-face listening, remember to maintain eye contact and to be and appear to be genuinely interested. Ask questions. Offer feedback with comments such as, "Go on," "I see," "Yes," "I understand," "That's interesting," "What else happened?" "Oh really," etc. Four of the magical listening phrases Tom Sullivan uses are:

1) "Say more about that..."
2) "Go into that some more..."
3) "Could you explain further..."
4) "Tell me more about that..."

When you use phrases like these, the other person knows you're listening!

Make up your mind that you are going to learn something from listening. Then, when you have listened, try to decide what you've learned from a particular conversation. If what you've learned is important enough, make some notes for future reference.

Above all, be patient, tolerant and understanding of other peoples' speaking habits. Some people may be shy, others perhaps not as eloquent as you, some slower in speech, and some with speech difficulties including ethnic or regional accents.

How successfully you network will depend upon how successfully you listen.

LISTENING FOR LEARNING

There is another form of networking listening – listening for learning. We're talking about listening to audio tapes on subjects pertinent to networking and listening to speakers whose topics address some aspects of the networking process. Some of the time you can use to listen to audio tapes is really free time. It's the time you spend driving – to work, for pleasure or while you're making your rounds. Hopefully you'll have a tape player in your car. If not, the price of a small portable player is a very worthwhile investment. Perhaps a word of caution is appropriate here. *Don't use a portable recorder with headphones while you're driving!* Other free time might be found during plane and train trips, while relaxing at home or while exercising.

Audio tapes are available on just about any subject that impacts on networking. Many of the tapes are reviewed in the monthly sales and marketing publications. Other sources are listed in the Tool Box section at the back of our book.

Seminars, workshops and luncheon and dinner speakers offer still another opportunity to listen and learn. Your local service clubs and Chambers of Commerce frequently offer speakers and programs with special emphasis on networking related subjects. Nationally known speakers are touring major cities regularly, and you can keep up with their appearances in your local newspapers or by watching your business mail.

Remember, how successfully you network depends on how successfully you listen. Fine tuning your listening skills will make a difference in your networking.

TEN SUGGESTIONS FOR LISTENING BETTER TO SPEAKERS

1. **Be rested** – To get the most out of any presentation you should be well rested. Dozing not only hinders what you can learn but is also impolite to the speaker.

2. **Arrive early** – You may get a chance to meet the speaker and to find a good seat – up front – where you will have good eye-contact.

3. **Be Alert** – Sit straight in your chair. Don't slouch. If you are at a desk, use it for note taking and not as a place to rest your elbows or head.

4. **Be prepared** – Have the materials you'll need. Don't depend on the sponsor to provide pencils and pads. Bring yours and be sure. Bring a small tape recorder, but make sure taping is permitted by the speaker.

5. **Be careful with notes** – It's good to take careful notes but you can become too absorbed in note taking and miss the message. Details and word-for-word notes are not as important as highlights.

6. **Give the speaker a break** – Try not to pre-judge the speaker because of dress, physical appearance, voice or mannerisms. What the speaker has to say should be of the most importance.

7. **Ask questions** – Most speakers allow time at the end of their presentations for questions from the floor. Don't be bashful. This is your opportunity to get the most from your investment and to get answers to those special questions you have.

8. Ask for a copy of the speech – Many speakers have copies of their speech with them or can send you one. If you are particularly anxious to access the entire speech, ask for a copy.

9. Meet the speaker – If, as suggested, you sat up front, you'll be able to be first in line to meet the speaker. You will be able to ask any personal questions you may have that you might not have wanted to ask from the floor. It is also your opportunity to say "thank you" or to make complimentary remarks.

10. Follow up – When you get back to the office or home, get your notes in order while things are still fresh in your memory. Plan how to specifically carry out those great ideas and suggestions you gleaned from the speaker's presentation.

ANNOYING LISTENING HABITS AS REPORTED BY A GROUP OF EXECUTIVES*

1. Lack of eye contact
2. Disagreeing with everything said.
3. Holding side conversations.
4. Correcting grammar or word choice.
5. Interrupting.
6. No response or feedback.
7. Having bad breath/sitting too close.
8. Completing sentence for person speaking.
9. Statements unrelated to the topic, or already answered questions.
10. Coughing or clearing the throat.
11. Answering before question is finished.
12. Allowing distractions to interfere.
13. Showing complete lack interest in what other person is saying.
14. Appearing impatient.
15. Ignoring other person to answer the phone.
16. Clipping fingernails.
17. Grooming – combing hair, putting on make-up.
18. Smoking.
19. Saying you understand when you don't; doing it wrong as result.
20. Blank stare.
21. Walking away but claiming to be listening.
22. Chewing gum.
23. Looking at your watch frequently.
24. Doodling.
25. Listening on the phone and asking you to keep talking.
26. Abruptly changing the subject.
27. Reading the mail, newspapers, magazines, reports, etc.
28. Shuffling papers.
29. Nervous mannerisms, fingertapping, twisting hair, knuckle cracking.
30. Using a speaker phone.

* Pat Payer/ Dr. Steven Boyd. Specialty Advertising Association International Seminar, "Effective Listening"

EIGHT LISTENING HABITS TO AVOID*

1. **Daydreaming:** Don't let your eyes wander or your head turn aimlessly about. Keep from drumming your fingers, snapping gum, mindlessly handling writing instruments, etc.

2. **Facts-only listening:** Facts are important, but only as stepping stones to ideas leading to major points. Don't keep your mind so occupied over minor tidbits that you miss the speaker's overall message.

3. **Poor posture:** Poor posture communicates poor listening; so don't slouch. The good listener's posture is alert, with eyes and attention concentrated on the speaker, regardless of whether the listener is standing or seated.

4. **Tuning out:** The burden of listening is on the listener. Don't automatically condemn a speaker or the subject as uninteresting; don't prejudice your listening because you don't like the speaker's looks, hair, voice, etc.

5. **Emotionalism:** Whatever your feelings about the speaker or his or her subject, hear the speaker out first. Don't allow yourself to become irritated or over-stimulated by what is said or how it is said – otherwise the message gets lost in the flash of emotions.

6. **Faking attention:** Don't pretend to be getting the message while your mind has made a mental detour and is busy with completely different ideas. If the speaker tries to interact with you at this point, you'll find yourself completely lost.

7. **Obsessive note-taking:** You can't try to write down, word for word, all that a speaker is saying and expect to hear the message. Just jot down the highlights or key ideas and pay more attention to hearing the message rather than trying to write down incomplete ideas.

8. **Time wasting:** Don't waste your listening time. You can listen faster than the speaker can speak, so anticipate the speakers points, evaluate and mentally summarize as your listen.

* Pat Payer/ Dr. Steven Boyd. Specialty Advertising Association International Seminar, "Effective Listening"

16

It's Show Time!

Trade show networking

Darrel J. Hamilton, Communications Director of the Trade Show Bureau, the trade show industry's association, reports that trade shows are the fastest growing segment of today's marketing mix.

Hamilton reports that there are approximately 8,000 trade and public shows in the United States each year and another 1,200 in Canada. Add to these numbers another 2,000 shows held by single companies (oil companies for their dealers, supermarket chains for their individual store buyers, brewers for their distributors, etc.).

Norman L. Abelson, author of ***Trade Show Basics,*** one of the few books dealing with trade shows, suggests that the trade show industry generates between $6 billion and $10 billion annually in the United States alone. He also estimates that approximately 50,000 companies exhibit, and over 35 million persons attend.

Trade shows are BIG business...and growing.

WHAT A PLACE TO NETWORK!

Keeping in mind the sheer size of trade shows, consider the tremendous opportunities for networking. Business people, professionals, hobbyists, volunteers – you name them – they all attend trade or public shows. At any time of the year there is a show of some kind held in virtually every city in the United States and Canada, ranging from a hobby or craft show to major industry shows.

These shows are divided into two basic groups, horizontal (wide appeal) shows and vertical (narrow focus) shows. The larger horizontal shows are typically consumer shows such as home improvement shows, flower shows, health shows and automobile shows. The vertical shows are industry oriented shows such as hardware shows, electronic shows and chemical shows.

Additionally we might add smaller shows like health fairs, state and local fairs, public service exhibits, hobby and special interest shows and craft fairs.

NETWORKING COMPONENTS OF TRADE SHOWS

Every trade show offers a wide variety of opportunities to network. Let's categorize the people attending a show for our networking purposes.

First there are the participants, and they fall into two groups. One group is the exhibitors; the other group consists of people attending to specifically visit the exhibitors on behalf of their company or other sponsor.

The next category would be people visiting for general interest on a more casual basis. Another category is a group of people who attend shows to find jobs or to pick up new lines. Lastly there are those that attend a show for the specific purpose of networking.

For each of these groups there are numerous ways and places to network.

NETWORKING THE SHOW

The obvious approach to networking a trade show is to just walk up and down aisles and see who you might meet. But there are other, less obvious, yet extremely effective approaches to networking the show.

For exhibitors, networking outside the booth can be almost as effective as the selling time in the booth. When booth personnel get a break they can network among other exhibitors who might be prospective customers. Michael J. Hatch, President of Professional Exhibits and Graphic Services, Inc. says in a brochure distributed by the Trade Show Bureau, "Review the exhibitor list. For many companies, the best prospects at the show can actually be some of your fellow exhibitors. If this is a possibility for you, make sure you allocate duty time for the sales people to 'walk the show' and visit with the other exhibitors, in addition to their booth assignments." You can also network with competitors or with industry people who might not come to your booth or display.

Other attendees can network for new ideas, new products, new jobs, or to meet both interesting and important new contacts.

"OFF THE FLOOR" NETWORKING

In addition to networking possibilities on the show floor, there are many other opportunities for networking "off the floor." Associated with most trade shows are receptions, cocktail parties, special meals and banquets, hospitality suites, training sessions and seminars. All of these events offer attendees a chance to network.

For those attending a show for more than one day and staying in a local hotel, there are more opportunities to network. The lobby of their hotel and the lobby of the official hotel provide great meeting places for making new friendships and greeting old friends and acquaintances.

A friend of ours takes particular advantage of hotel lobbies for his networking. He stands or sits in a spot where he can see who comes off the elevators. He can quickly zero in on those people he is especially anxious to see during the show.

When a trade show offers sponsored transportation, usually a bus that makes a loop among the major hotels, we always skip the cab and ride the bus – not to save money, but rather to increase our chances to network. Not unlike airplanes or trains, trade show busses often put you in the right place with the right people at the right time.

Another friend of ours tells the story of having a new product from Europe he wanted to introduce into the United States. While riding a show bus from his hotel to the Advertising Specialty Show in Chicago, he wound up in the seat next to the marketing manager of a major US supplier of products similar to the imported item our friend wanted to promote. By the time the bus reached its destination, a tentative deal was set up for the supplier to introduce the new product in this country...and the bus ride was free.

An unusual but effective place for trade show networking is in the airport prior to boarding your plane to the show or following the show. You'll find plenty of attendees in the executive lounges of the major airlines.

TWO BIRDS WITH ONE TRIP

It seems almost too obvious to mention, but a trip to a trade show away from home provides an already paid trip to also visit people in your network in the city of the show. Along with planning your work at the show, side visits require equal planning to get the most out of the spare time you have available. It may mean calling friends ahead of time to get them to meet you or to arrange for you to seek them out for a meeting.

TRADE SHOWS ARE A MUST

For the serious networker, we have three basic trade show rules :

1. Attend trade shows wherever and whenever you can.
2. Plan ahead to take advantage of every opportunity to network the show – don't leave it to chance.
3. Follow up after the show.

Perhaps the most serious problem with attending trade shows is apathy on the part prospective attendees. Their big questions are: "What can I get out of the show for the time and money spent?"; "Will I sell more product?"; "Will I find something that will pay for my trip?"

If you consider serious networking as an integral and vital part of your show trip, the answer to these questions will surely be positive.

To learn how trade shows helped someone network their way to success, see Success Story #4 about Joyce Werkman.

TEN NETWORKING TIPS FOR TRADE SHOWS

1. **Plan ahead –** check the exhibitors directory and map out an aisle and booth route that assures you of seeing the people most important to you.

2. **Carry a miniature tape recorder –** or at least a small note book to capture thoughts in the fast paced atmosphere of the trade show.

3. **Bring plenty of business cards –** really more than you think you'll need (and you'll still probably run short).

4. **Make notes –** on the back of the business cards you collect.

5. **Avoid carrying bags** – of catalogs, literature, samples. Ask suppliers to mail these things to you following the show.

6. **Avoid extensive booth conversations –** which might be a distraction from customers and prospects being seen. If you want more than a brief networking encounter, set up an appointment during the show.

7. **Get some rest –** and check your grooming several times during the show day. Your networking will surely reflect your attitude and appearance as the day wears on.

8. **Organize –** your cards and notes at the end of every day. Outline the action you are going to take following the show.

9. **Use the show as an opportunity –** to send post cards to key people in your network.

10. **Follow up –** with important contacts just as soon as you get back home or to the office.

17

Networking "By the Book"

Send me a person who reads

A great ad campaign of several years ago was based on the headline "Send Me A Man Who Reads." The campaign extolled the virtues of reading. As with the famous ***Wall Street Journal*** ads, the campaign suggested that reading, and particularly reading the right things, was a golden road to success and happiness. The campaign was sponsored by International Paper Company (who today would certainly change the headline to "Send Me A *Person* Who Reads"). They naturally wanted you to buy books, which were hopefully, and probably, made from their fine papers.

Today, when we want to add interesting and exciting people to our network we would certainly include someone who is an active reader.

WHY READING IS SO IMPORTANT

Newspapers, books and magazines not only contain the expected news, information and enjoyment items but most of all they're chock-full of *ideas* – ideas you can use every day in your networking communications. In your daily reading you should be able to augment the networking tools discussed in this book.

With a planned reading program, hardly a day will go by without something for you to learn about direct mail, public relations, speaking, organizations, speakers and the many other topics that are so vital to good networking.

Additionally, reading printed news media will provide insights into people with whom you might want to purposely network. Remember Ken Erdman's dedication in the front of this book to Murray Raphel? Ken met Murray as a result of reading Murray's magazine column. Remember Don Craighead, the person to whom Tom Sullivan dedicated this book? Don was so impressed with Tom's book, ***Network Your Net Worth***, he contacted Tom in order to add him to *his* network.

Both of these meetings are typical examples of networking from the written word.

WHAT SHOULD YOU READ?

A basic reading list should contain your hometown newspapers along with a good national newspaper. We suggest the ***Wall Street Journal*** or the Sunday edition of the ***New York Times***, the ***Chicago Tribune***, or the ***San Francisco Chronicle***, depending upon which part of the country you live in. Next on our list is a good weekly news magazine such as ***Time*** or ***Newsweek***. Then we suggest a business publication such as ***Business Week***, ***Forbes*** or perhaps ***Fortune*** magazine. The publications for your trade, business or special interest should also be included. And, if you can squeeze them in, your local newspaper, a local business publication and a local "big city" magazine are good sources of information.

Books, of course, are important to your networking knowledge. In addition to books specifically on networking, you'll want to keep up-to-date on other books related in some way to the networking process.

It hardly seems necessary to say "read your mail" but we mean *all* of your mail – including the advertising mail. Often your advertising mail will produce great ideas and concepts that can help you in your reading. Announcements of new books and other publications that might be of interest could very well be found in your mailbox.

GET HELP

If you say, "Oh, this all sounds great, but I don't have time to do all of this reading," it's time to look for help.

If you are fortunate enough to have a secretary ask him or her to scan at least some of your reading for items that might be of interest to you. After all, your secretary should know what would be of interest or importance to you. Next ask business people working with or for you to note items in publications that might be of interest. Lastly encourage those in your network to keep an eye out for news about those things about which you're particularly concerned.

WHAT DO YOU DO WITH WHAT YOU FIND?

Networking from reading requires some tools. You may want to carry a highlighter pen to mark things of interest, along with a small pair of scissors or a clipping tool to cut from magazines or papers. Or you may just want to tear out pages for future filing.

A filing system, however minimal, is a must. Good networkers always have a file of helpful information. Perhaps baseball's most famous promoter, Bill Veek of the Chicago White Sox, cataloged his ideas on 3" X 5" cards. It's guessed that his files are worth a fortune to any team. With the newest software for lap- and desktop computers, you can find a program that will provide for note taking and an easy-to-retrieve information system.

YOUR LIBRARY CARD

Somebody once said, "Your library card is your passport to success," and we believe it might be. Probably too few people take full advantage of the great facilities available at most libraries. For networking, the library is an invaluable reference source, particularly for names and addresses of people you might want to contact. And remember, most libraries can be accessed by phone for reference information you might need.

Reading is a way to cultivate your mind as well as your network. Remember the headline we mentioned at the beginning of this chapter. To be a good networker – and to be someone others want to network with – be a person who reads.

See the "Toolbox Section" at the back of the book for a networking reading list.

Part Three

Bringing In Your Catch

The Techniques of Networking

18

The Nine Magic Words of Networking

"I have a problem and I need your help"

Over and over again we read or hear stories in the media about how people unexpectedly come to the aid of others. The stories range from life-saving super heroism to acts of charity for someone whose plight has caught the attention of the public.

Behind the scenes, however, people are continually helping each other in smaller, unpublicized ways. The help can come as individual help, corporate help or social help.

At the individual level, help varies, ranging from small courtesies to offering support for someone's more specific needs. At the corporate level the help may address employee needs or approach community problems in conjunction with others. At the social level, organizations such as service clubs and volunteer groups are continually offering aid.

PEOPLE REALLY DO WANT TO HELP

We believe, and have found, that most people really do want to be helpful to others. Sometimes a crisis situation presents itself where help is needed and you are there and available to help. A recent example is the story of friends, a husband and wife, who visited New York City for an evening of opera and dinner. While walking from dinner, the husband collapsed and fell to the sidewalk on his face. From many of the stories we've all read about the wild streets of the Big Apple, we might have expected the worst to happen. Perhaps rowdies rushing to strip the wallet from our friend's pocket.

Instead, passers-by stopped to offer whatever assistance they could to the couple. Several people ran to telephone for help or to seek police help. Even a "tough" New York cabbie pulled over to offer a ride to the hospital. None of these people were consciously looking for a chance to be helpful – instead the opportunity arose and was acted upon.

We now have a new respect for the people of New York.

The help mentioned above is generally unsolicited help. But what about asking for help? Is this a sign of weakness? Will people be offended by a request for help? What are your chances of getting help when you really need it? Is there a networking technique that you can use?

THE NINE MAGIC WORDS OF NETWORKING

Some years ago we discovered nine magic words, what we now call our Nine Magic Words of Networking.

Here they are: **"I have a problem and I need your help."**

The power of these words is absolutely amazing. Time and time again we have purposely used the technique of approaching people for help with this short, to the point sentence. And it works!

The words get attention. They particularly appeal to people's desire to be helpful. They preface your needs simply and politely. People want to believe that they are problem solvers. And they help you.

Several years ago we tried an experiment to prove our point. We needed some clippings from recent issues of our local newspaper, and we sent our summer intern to the publisher's office to ask for copies of the desired material.

Our intern's mission was not as simple as it seemed. Previous encounters with the paper's receptionist had convinced us that she was not an easy person to deal with. She was perhaps not ideally suited to be a receptionist! Although we had never approached her with a request for clippings, we were sure that her response to the request would be less than enthusiastic.

But before our intern left on his errand, we told him he should introduce himself and his company, then immediately use the magic words and tell the receptionist what he wanted.

We could hardly wait to find out what had happened. "No problem," he said upon his return. "She gave me *two* copies of what you wanted – and she even suggested that the next time I need copies I call ahead so that she could have the material ready when I arrived."

MONEY IN YOUR POCKET

Write down the nine magic words. Tuck them into your wallet or purse. They might just be one of the most important things you'll learn from our book.

19

Finding A New Job

Career networking

As this chapter is being written, the jobless rate in America has climbed to 5.8% for adult women and 6.4% for adult men. Each day's newspapers announce new layoffs at major corporations and small companies alike. There seem to be more people looking for jobs than at any time in our memory.

Perhaps you are one of them. Or you may suspect that you are about to lose your job. Or you may be thinking about making a career change. In any of these situations you'll need to use *every marketing tool available* to attain one of the most important successes in your contemporary life – a new job.

CAREER NETWORKING

Typical approaches to job-hunting include reading help wanted ads, sending inquiry letters with resumes to prospective employers and contacting employment agencies. We believe that networking may be an even more important, effective and successful tool. According to Emily Koltnow and Lynne S. Dumas, authors of ***Congratulations! You've Been Fired!***, approximately four out of every five jobs are filled through personal contact. Through networking we'll believe you'll reach people who might not only know of job openings, but might also be in a position to get you an interview or support your job application personally.

Job consultant Marvin Walberg of Birmingham, Alabama had this to say in a Scripps Howard News Service article:

"The most successful method of job searching is networking. So you've heard. But exactly what is networking? Think of it as skipping stones over a calm lake surface. Each time the stone touches down, it leaves a ripple on the water. Each ripple grows larger, gently making contact with the nearest ripple. The contacts continues until a large area of the lake surface is involved.

"You, like the stone, network when you skip from contact to contact, leaving ripples of information about yourself as you go – information about your experience, goals and interests. At the same time, you receive ripples of information about people, industries, jobs, careers.

"You take these ripples of information and continue networking on and on until you find yourself in front of someone who sees you as a solution to a need – a need that may not have existed before you started networking."

WHERE TO NETWORK

In a word, EVERYWHERE!

Stories abound about where and how people found jobs though networking. One of our favorites is about someone we know. This man had sold his small electronics distributorship and had been retired for about six months. He was bored. He started networking through business friends, customers and suppliers telling them that he wanted (a) a nine to five job, (b) not too much responsibility and (c) a job where he could use his electronic parts experience. These criteria are certainly not easy to match, even though he was not looking for a substantial salary.

On a Monday our friend phoned a salesperson who used to call on him. "Keep your eyes out for me," he said. "Maybe you may come across someone who could use me." On Wednesday the salesperson was in a customer's office. During the meeting the customer asked the salesperson, "Do you, by chance, know of anybody who might be looking for a telephone sales job? I need someone with some electronics experience for a strictly 9 to 5 job, with few responsibilities – but I can't afford to pay much." By Friday a networking match-up had been made and our retired friend was at work in his new job.

Our story may sound almost unbelievable, but it's the kind of job networking story that's repeated over and over again. Getting your story out to EVERYBODY is the answer.

Who is EVERYBODY?

If there is a weakness in the networking process, that weakness is shortsightedness on the part of networkers. We fail to consider all of the people with whom we can network. This is particularly true with job-seeking – a process which is frequently time-sensitive. You've lost your job. You expect to lose your job. You're forced into early retirement. You're about to graduate with no significant job prospects. You've had to close your business. Bleak as these possibilities sound, they describe the situations of acquaintances of ours this very year. These people need a job NOW. But where to look?

To find a job or embark on a new career you have to network with *everybody* and you can't forget *anybody.* This concept takes you beyond the networks we've suggested you build, earlier in our book.

In job prospecting you have to consider everyone with whom you come in contact as a potential networker – someone else who might help you find a new job. Though not intended as a complete list, the following suggestions should give you some insight into who you should be networking with in your job search:

- your family
- your friends
- fellow employees
- employees of suppliers
- employees of competitors

- church friends
- country club members
- hobbyists
- fellow sports people
- the retailers you support
- your service station
- your barber
- college and high school alumnae
- fraternity or sorority friends
- civic and service club members
- the person next to you on the plane, train or bus
- your insurance agent
- your stockbroker
- your teachers
- your elected officials
- the head of your chamber of commerce

You get the idea – EVERYBODY!

Now transfer this list to a notebook and start to build on it. Put check marks next to each entry after a successful networking attempt. This will be a good scorecard for your efforts.

YOUR BEST PROSPECTS

Your EVERYBODY list can be refined. There are those among your prospects who are more likely to be helpful than others. For these contacts you'll have to set up a special agenda and single these people out for special attention.

- **People in your close network** – friends, family, Mentors, Librarians, Advocates and, above all, your Superknots.

- **Influential people** – people who head up businesses, organizations, political parties, etc. The use of an influential person's name in an introduction will act as a reference for you.

- **People in the business or industry in which you have a particular interest** – start where you want to go. Make as many contacts as you can with people in companies, trade associations and other organizations in your field of special interest. Don't be afraid to telemarket yourself. Make cold calls and let people know you are available.

WHERE THE DUCKS ARE FLYING

There's an old axiom that says, "If you want to shoot ducks, go where the ducks are flying." The same holds true for job-hunting. Often finding the people you'll want to network with will require looking in special places. Here are just a few suggestions for where to look:

- trade shows
- conventions
- your church
- networking groups
- civic and social club meetings
- alumnae meetings
- class reunions
- jobless support groups
- business card exchange groups

How do you find these groups and discover where they meet? Easy. Most major city newspapers run bulletin board sections once a week (usually in their Sunday edition). Or you can try the yellow pages of your phone book.

If your song has been "Don't Get Around Much Any More," it's time to change your tune. You had better get around – a lot more!

HOW TO NETWORK YOUR WAY TO A NEW JOB

Networking for a new job is not casual networking. For the process to be really effective you must go back to the first word in our definition of networking – disciplined. To be successful you'll need to use every networking technique possible.

Each chapter in this book impacts upon your job search. Some chapters enlarge on the ideas we present in this particular chapter. Also, you'll read, in-depth, about using the phone, writing letters, researching in the library, asking for help, using "magic" words, establishing a database to record both potential and already contacted prospects and how to use your business card. If you read this chapter first, be assured there's more help, much more, throughout our book.

LETTERS OF INTRODUCTION

We believe that one of the best ways to get an interview is with your own letter of introduction. It will precede the sending of your resume. It should tell who you are, what you can do, promote some of your strengths, (benefits to the employer) and "ask for the order" – create enough curiosity to get the prospect to want to contact you for your resume, or ask you for an interview.

These letters can be mailed on a selective basis, going at first only to those who you think will have an active interest in you. Next you can do an entire direct mail program, mailing to as many as many people as you can comfortably manage.

YOUR RESUME

Time, effort and money are all well spent on your resume. Though its importance will differ from prospect to prospect, rest assured that a professionally designed and written resume is one of the most effective tools in your quest for employment.

Your resume can be handled in two ways. You can tackle it as a do-it-yourself project. (A word of warning here: because of the importance of your resume, if you are going to do it yourself, please get help from books on resume writing at your bookstore or local library.) Your second choice is to have your resume done by a professional. If you can afford to do this, the investment is well worth the money you spend.

YOUR BUSINESS CARD

A business card is an accepted tool of professional and social etiquette. When seeking employment you should have your own business card with all of the necessary information needed for a prospective employer to have readily available when the need arises to contact you.

Plain business cards without illustrations or artwork are satisfactory and inexpensive. The quality can vary depending on your budget, but you'll be better perceived with something more than the least expensive card.

Be sure to include several of your business cards in any correspondence you send to prospective employers. That way, they can keep one for themselves and perhaps pass the others on. Give your cards out to everybody you meet (and that means EVERYBODY). Don't be bashful – give more than one to each person. You might make a handwritten note on the back of the card mentioning that you are on a job search. That way, the recipients will be less likely to forget where and why they received your card.

TELEMARKETING

Before you find a job you may find a telephone receiver growing out of your ear. The telephone is the networking tool you'll use the most. To get the most benefit from the use of your phone you should follow some basic rules for disciplined networking calls. They include:

1. Set up an efficient phone desk. Have your tools handy: appropriate phone books, pencils, pens and paper, a clock and your database.

2. Do basic research and preparation before you make your call. Know something about the person your are going to call. Have written objectives – know what you are going to say and how you are going to say it.

3. Pause before you dial. Are you ready? Do you know how you are going to start your conversation? Are you prepared to speak with authority? Be careful of your voice. Not too loud, not too soft, not too fast and not too slow. Well then, what do you do? Communications experts suggest that you try to match the tone and speed of voice to that of the person on the other end of the phone.

4. Be prepared for rejection. Sorry to say, but that's what you'll get on most of your calls. Know how you'll handle the initial rejection, create a situation where you can go back to the same persons again if you didn't get them the first time or if you received a negative response.

5. Avoid idle chatter. Recognize that people's time is limited and that you are imposing on them. Get to the point quickly, but don't rush your presentation.

6. Set goals. Know exactly what you want to accomplish on each call. Ask for the order – try to accomplish what you had set as your goal(s).

7. Listen carefully. A rejection might come with suggestions for other places to try. Or, with careful listening you may detect that a rejection is not final. Remember that talking *too* much can sometimes lead to you talking yourself *out* of a potential winning situation.

8. Follow up and follow through. Every phone call has the potential for some action. If you make promises, keep them promptly. If you're told to call back remember to call back. If nothing substantial happens initially, consider what a call-back might accomplish.

9. Make notes in your desk diary or database of what happened with each call. You'll be amazed at how helpful this information will be at a later time.

10. Remember to say "thank you" even if you get turned down. And add, "Keep me in mind if the situation changes." Remember, not every person interviewed will make a lasting impression. Most employers don't forget appreciation expressed, particularly by applicants who have been turned down.

REFERENCES, ENDORSEMENTS & TESTIMONIALS

Second party references, endorsements and testimonials have a lot of impact. When networking, try not only to get leads, interviews and a chance to mail a resume, but find people who know you and will be willing to say something good about you.

Your very best results may come if you can have someone "at the top" pass along a recommendation to someone at a lower level.

RESEARCH NETWORKING

The more you know about a prospective employer, the better your chances of getting a job. Researching a target company is both necessary and detailed. You'll want to do the obvious library work, checking on financial directories, annual reports and news items. But don't forget to use your network to get personal information about the company and its officers before you make your first contacts.

We have a friend who, when being interviewed, was told by the vice-president of the company, "You know more about my company than I do." Our friend got the job.

MOTIVATION

When you're in the job market the chances for disappointment and discouragement are ever present. Consider your networking as a competitive endeavor. How many letters can you write today? How many phone calls? How many appointments can you get? How many answers can you get to your letters? How many supporters can you find? Just as with a competitive sport, keep records. Reward yourself for small victories. Celebrate bigger victories.

Convince yourself that you *will* get a job. You *can* network your way to success.

20

Networking in the Work Place

Moving up the corporate ladder

Why network in the work place? Reasons include striving for increased compensation, aspiring for a personal promotion, contributing to the overall success of the business or seeking better working conditions.

A WARNING

Just as moving up in your company can be significantly aided by networking practices, the potential for creating problems (and possible enemies) is equally significant. In the work place, networking can be used in a positive manner, but special attention must be paid to business ethics and personal morality.

The temptation to overdo the use of networking to take advantage of your co-workers is always present, though not always intended. Fairness and objectivity are the watchwords; the Golden Rule is *the* rule!

UP THE LADDER AND *DOWN* THE LADDER

If not a warning, perhaps at least a word of caution, is appropriate in any discussion of work place networking.

The most obvious directions to network are either sideways or upward. After all, what can those *beneath* you do to help your cause? Plenty! In fact, many of those beneath you can be your best sources and resources of help and information. As you move up in any organization you need the support of those that work both with and for you. Effective networking can help you immensely in gaining support from fellow workers.

SANDY'S STORY

Sandy Bennett started out in business the hard way. When her husband became disabled without warning, she assumed responsibility for four children. She was widowed at age forty for the second time, and she started in the job market without a college degree. Her first job was an entry level position as a billing clerk. From there she moved up to operations manager of a $75 million corporation – in just seven years.

Her secret? Networking in her work place.

The important strength she brought to her first job was an involvement in, and dedication to, community service. She has served as a board member or officer of a wide variety of community philanthropic and service organizations. The positions she has held include corporate donations chairperson for a children's home, President of the greater Minneapolis Federation of Women's clubs and President of a Toastmasters group. She is also involved in her community college women's resource center.

From these varied experiences she forged her personal networking philosophy. What's the problem and how can I help? (Notice the "how can I help" instead of the "how can you help me" approach.)

A TYPICAL WORK PLACE NETWORK

A typical example of a workplace network comes from Donna Lucas who has worked for the St. Paul Pioneer Press newspaper for more than 13 years.

As an advertising salesperson for the paper she has frequent opportunities to network with fellow employees and with project co-workers outside the paper. A major city newspaper provides a huge potential for a multi-level networking system. From Donna's position she, like many in larger businesses, networks vertically and horizontally – with her personal bosses or subordinates, or with those at any level in other departments.

"In the high pressure and fast paced business of imparting information to literally hundreds of thousands of people every single day, you are in a networking wonderland," says Donna. "Here the Rolodex® is as important as the daily weather report – the positive interaction between people is essential."

CELEBRITY NETWORKING

Donna's workplace networking contacts have given her the opportunity to meet both the famous and the near famous.

When NBC had a film crew in her town to do a local news story, Donna, through her network, met one of their cameramen. They had similar business interests and Donna added him to her network and kept in touch with him.

Several years later the cameraman was back in town to film a new NBC television show with a nationally famous woman interviewer interviewing an equally famous celebrity. As a result of Donna's networking contact with the cameraman, she was invited to the filming and had the pleasure of lunching with the two celebrities.

Just another example of the exciting opportunities available in building a network in your own workplace.

TEN SUGGESTIONS FOR WORK PLACE NETWORKING

1. Do the very best job possible in all of your endeavors. You have to be effective in your own job if you want others to follow and help.

2. Maintain a caring attitude to both co-workers and superiors. Realize that everyone is working toward a common goal.

3. Don't be afraid to befriend superiors. Once they recognize you're truly interested in helping them reach a common goal, an atmosphere of trust will develop.

4. Look at the overall picture. Learn as much as you can about the company and how each area functions. This is accomplished by networking with other employees in other departments. Find out about their duties, their goals, their frustrations and problems as well as their hopes and dreams.

5. Once you know the company and the people, **match people and their expertise** to solve problems through networking.

6. Identify individual skills and talents in other people. Use a networking catalog system to keep track of this knowledge. You'll become a resource person – a problem solver. ("Ask Sandy, she'll know who can help.") John D. Spooner, author of ***Smart People*** coined the term "Lamplighters" to describe problem solvers. The "Lamplighters" in companies are the people who get the promotions.

7. Follow up and follow through! Once you have initiated a solution to a problem, check back with the people involved and see how things turned out and how else you might be of help.

8. Find out your organization's most pressing problems. Analyze possible solutions. Create specific plans to address the problems. Two of Sandy's promotions came when she discovered problems in her company and proposed new concepts to address them.

9. Network with everyone, no matter what their position. This can also be called being a friend – but it's not necessary to develop a close friendship. It's simply a matter of being friendly and being willing to help.

Saying hello, smiling and just being concerned about your fellow workers takes only a few seconds and can make a big difference in their day (and yours). The higher you climb in an organization the more valuable this skill becomes.

10. Participate in company sponsored events. Picnics, sports and social events, charitable drives, educational seminars, field trips and company sponsored clubs are all ways to network. If your company doesn't offer any of these activities, seek permission to start one. Nobody said you can't be an assertive networker.

It can only be to your benefit to cultivate a work place network. And remember, what you bring to your network will certainly affect the benefits you derive from it.

21

The Social Scene

Networking for friendships

Social networking, whether for platonic friendships, a spouse, or to increase our network of really close friends, utilizes most of our available networking opportunities.

Social networking stands apart from networking for business or professional purposes. In social networking the goals are not for numbers of leads or lists of prospects, "signed-up" customers, new clients or new patients. Social networking, however, is still very much success oriented.

For some readers, the ability to successfully network for new personal relationships might be their only goal. If you are networking for a spouse, and find one, you can certainly consider that you've networked your way to success!

A DIFFERENT CAST OF CHARACTERS

In business and professional networking, the people involved tend to already have some experience and know-how in meeting and interacting with strangers. They have developed basic networking techniques because of their job experiences. In the social scene – the search for new friends – many of the participants are shy and hesitant to extend themselves. Hopefully, this chapter will help both the aspiring networker and the networkers with some experience who wants to reach further.

WHAT'S YOUR NAME?

The basic, level one networking technique is to extend ourselves – to *start* a conversation.

When you were four years old you were probably an excellent level one networker. You knew how to ask those outrageously personal, conversation starting questions:

> What's your name?
> How old are you?
> Where do you live?
> What do your Mommy and Daddy do?
> Do you want to play?
> Can I come over to your house?

I guess we can remember that far back. Why did we then seem to have the natural attributes of good networkers but never continued to progress? Then we were innocent! We hadn't been conditioned to the consequences of extending ourselves. We were soon warned of the dangers of talking to strangers. "Children should be seen and not heard," is a principle our parents might have observed. "Mind your manners," we were told.

Robert Fulghum, author of the immensely popular book, ***All I Ever Needed to Know I Learned in Kindergarten,*** sold hundreds of thousands copies by telling his readers how basic lessons, learned in kindergarten, can serve you well in later life.

GETTING READY FOR SOCIAL ENCOUNTERS

Before we review where to do our social networking let's think about how to do it. Important considerations include:

1) How to overcome fear of rejection

2) How to greet people effectively
3) How to get ready for conversations
4) How to start a conversation
5) How to develop friendships

FEAR OF REJECTION

Probably a book could (or has been) written on fear of rejection. For the purposes of networking in the social scene, fear of rejection usually manifests itself in the fear of meeting strangers...a fear of being rejected by them. Fear of rejection is an acquired fear.

Psychologists tell us that as babies we really only had two fears, fear of falling and fear of loud noises. For most people, many acquired fears can be conquered. Here are some suggestions for conquering fear of rejection.

Recognize that fear of rejection keeps you from extending yourself in new situations and when meeting new people. Next recognize that probably 95% of the time your initiatives to meet new people will succeed. Remember kindergarten. Don't be afraid of strangers (meeting new people). Understand that other people are as eager to make new friends as you are. Do you have any idea how relieved and grateful other people are going to feel because you took the initiative and started a conversation? Believe in yourself, you really have something to offer a new acquaintance. You can be a good listener.

Lastly, your chances for success can be substantially improved by *preparing* to meet new people. This calls for doing some homework to be ready to engage in sparkling conversation – the kind that will surely win you new friends.

GETTING READY FOR A CONVERSATION

Try these suggestions to improve your conversational skills:

A) Find three interesting, stimulating or exciting things that have happened to you recently. Be prepared to relate them in story form. Above all put your feelings into them.

B) As you read books, magazines, newspapers, take special note of general interest items that you can share in conversations with others.

C) When you have seen good movies, TV, plays or theater, your recommendation to a new friend may carry more weight than a professional reviewer.

D) If you have trouble remembering jokes, next time you hear one you'd like to share, jot it down.

E) Offering insights on current events can result in stimulating conversation as long as your comments informed and general. As soon as you express too strong a view, you run the risk of finding opposition. This often stops conversation instantly!

F) Express a sincere interest in the other person's adventures, families, hobbies, sightseeing, surgeries, travels.

G) Use the other person's name in conversation. They love to hear it, and it helps you to fix it in your memory.

H) Be prepared. Your next conversation may begin today or tonight.

GREETING PEOPLE

Greeting someone for the first time gives you that important opportunity to make a good first impression. The greeting is perhaps the most important part of face-to-face networking. So be alert, be courteous, smile and shake hands.

The handshake is very important. It should be done with a firm grip, but not be bone-crushing or finger-squeezing. It should be short, perhaps no longer than 5 or 6 seconds. Some people like to enlarge on the typical handshake by placing their left hand over the clasped right hand, or use their left hand to hold the other person's elbow. Remember, however, that when you are shaking hand you are invading the other persons *personal* space. (Personal space is an arm's length away.) Unless you have reason to believe that you won't be offensive with something more than the typical handshake, it's better to be safe than sorry.

If you are in a social situation where you might have a cold and wet glass in your hand, or you hands might be damp from perspiration, be sure to have a napkin or handkerchief handy to be able to discreetly dry your hands. Nobody likes to shake a cold, clammy hand.

A woman should extend her hand when being introduced or greeting someone. Men should wait for a woman's extended hand before offering to shake hands. Remember to shake hands when ending a conversation or meeting.

STARTING A CONVERSATION

Meeting people seems to come naturally to some of us. To others, it seems like work. In either case, it requires one person to initiate the conversation. But how do we think up something that doesn't sound trite? The answer is the key word – sincerity. If it originates with you and sounds like the way you would say it, then it is going to sound sincere, not trite.

What is there to talk about? The list is endless. Here are some ice-breakers that will easily open up a conversation:

A) Share views about everyday life. Probe to find out what common areas of interest you may have: early childhood, schools, where you were born, likes and dislikes.

B) Search for things like: Are you from Florida, Texas, Maine, etc.? What city? Where do you work? What's your name? That's an interesting name. Is it Irish?

C) Comment on the surroundings – the room, the furniture, pictures, the yard.

D) Compliments – say something complimentary about the person's appearance, hobby, family, etc.

E) Discover the personality make-up. Is the person married or single? Do they like parties? Are they an interesting person? Bold? Shy? Quiet? Smiling?

F) Ask practical questions – May I get you a drink? Do you mind if I sit next to you? Do you attend many of these functions? Are you a regular member?

G) Share a funny personal story.

H) Ask questions like:

- What's new in your life?
- What's happening in your world?
- How's your day going, or how did your day go?
- Do you know what I learned (or did, or saw) today?

I) Discuss hobbies – knitting, horseback riding, canoeing, hiking, jogging, fishing, camping, dancing.

J) Can you tell me who your dentist is? Who repairs your car? Where did you buy that outfit?

K) You remind me of my brother, sister; he/she had a similar interest.

L) Current events – sports, politics, general interest news, major issues.

M) Directions – How do I get home from here? Do you live close by?

As your conversation develops, be alert for opportunities to help. For instance some of the best ways to get the other person's attention are:

a) I know where you can get that.
b) I know who you should call or see.
c) You should get in contact with.
d) Let me see if I can help.

Who wouldn't be drawn to leads that would ease their life, or solve a nagging problem? And you were the one that put them on to it! Along with the instant gratification you feel that comes with helping, there is also a desire on their part to be helpful in return.

DEVELOPING FRIENDSHIPS

Here again is a topic worthy of an entire book. (Remember Dale Carnegie's ***How To Win Friends And Influence People.***) We have a few tips that will at least help in your quest for new friends.

First read one or more books on how to develop friends. We certainly recommend Dale Carnegie's book (see the reading list at back of this book). Make a definite commitment to make friends. Make yourself available by being in situations where you can meet new people. When you have made an acquaintance that you would like to develop into a friendship, take the initiative. *You* make the phone calls or write the notes. *You* extend the invitations. Stay in contact. Friendships require closeness. Keep your promises. Be helpful. Share problems. (A problem shared is a problem solved.) Be trustworthy. Don't be afraid to ask for help. (See Chapter 18, *The Nine Magic Words of Networking*.) Don't be afraid to express your feelings toward your friends – people want to know that they are appreciated. Above all, remember the Golden Rule: "Do unto others as you would have them do unto you."

WHERE TO NETWORK SOCIALLY

Throughout our book you'll read in depth about the many places to meet for business or professional networking. Many of these same places will obviously work just as well for your social networking. For this chapter we list some of the places considered in other chapters and add a few that are particularly appropriate to social networking.

PLACES TO NETWORK SOCIALLY

1. Your house of worship
2. Service clubs
3. Hobby clubs
4. Sports groups
5. Political functions
6. Networking groups
7. Chambers of Commerce
8. Health clubs
9. College functions
10. Singles groups
11. YMCA/YWCA
12. Historical societies
13. Veterans groups
14. Travel tours
15. Parent/teacher groups
16. Educational courses
17. Library activities
18. Choral groups
19. Little theater groups
20. Volunteer groups

The number of friends you have is only limited by the effort you make to gain them. And remember, nobody can have too many friends.

The Seven Deadly Sins of Social Networking

1. **Failing to set a goal.** Before stepping through the door, a networker should know who's going to be there, who he or she wants to meet and have made arrangements to be introduced. The networker who doesn't do this will have nothing better to do than sample the hors d'oeuvres and in the long run will have accomplished nothing.

2. **Finding someone you know and clinging to that person throughout the evening.** This just isn't profitable in terms of building business. If you're there to work the room, work it. As a networker, imagine you're the host instead of a guest. Introduce yourself and introduce other guests to each other.

3. **Hiding yourself in a corner, hoping the world will come to you.** It generally won't. The best place to station oneself is just to the left of the door inside the room. It's a proven fact that people tend to drift to their left as they enter. When they do, be sure to say hello.

4. **Passing the very people you're there to meet, like ships in the night.** If planned introductions fail to materialize, networkers should introduce themselves. A simple technique is to get close, wait for an opportune moment, then put out your hand. Tell them you've been looking forward to meeting them. Tell them you've admired their company, or a certain product, or the way they've marketed it. Most people are flattered to have their work recognized, and that will start the conversational ball rolling. You don't have to push hard, but you do have to break that inertia.

5. **Being inattentive.** In their desire to circulate, some people keep their eyes wandering around the room, obviously looking for the next target of opportunity. Instead, they need to focus on the person they're talking to, not beyond his or her shoulder. To do anything else in unnerving, impolite, and counter productive. When the conversation is over, that's the time to say goodbye and start circulating again.

6. **Overstaying one's one welcome.** Good networkers (like all good guests) know when to leave. You don't necessarily have to be the first to leave, but you should never be the last.

7. **Failing to follow up.** This is perhaps the deadliest of the seven sins of social networking. If you make a promise to call on Monday, do it! If a certain article or report discussed over the crab canape´ has been promised, it must be sent! Otherwise, the credibility the networker has worked so hard to establish is lost, and the whole encounter will have been a wash.

***Contributor: David Dworski**, networker, head of Santa Monica, CA consulting firm Dworski & Associates, and creator of a sales seminar series entitled, "Working with Energy."*

22

Join The Club

Professional networking groups

In recent years specific groups, clubs, and associations have been formed for the express purpose of helping their members network with each other. Some of the groups have been formed to develop networks of business contacts. Others exist as self-help groups or support groups using networking techniques to accomplish their goals. Still others meet in a structured way to share knowledge or skills.

Let's take a look at several unique and successful groups and learn how they use a formal structure to help network their way to success.

"AFTER HOURS" NETWORKING

Perhaps the most best known and most popular structured networking groups are those sometimes called "after hours" get togethers or business card exchanges or "swaps." These groups most often are not stand-alone groups but are sponsored by some other larger and more generalized organization. Typically it might be a local Chamber of Commerce, Visitor and Convention Bureau, YMCA/YWCA, or a business, social or civic club.

The format is informal. Most often the sponsoring organization provides a meeting place for an after-hour gathering. Refreshments are often included, either with or without cost to the attendees, and of course, the most important element of all is provided – the name tag.

Beyond that, the networking is up to those who attend, with little help from the sponsors. The idea is to socialize, to meet people in an atmosphere where everyone knows that they are expected to communicate with total strangers for the express purpose of satisfying some networking need.

The participants bring that essential networking tool to the meeting – their business cards.

Let the networking begin!

Those who participate in these after-hours gatherings vary in their networking intensity, from casual to aggressive to overbearing. The results most often reflect the networking approach. The business card exchange concept has many pluses. It provides both the place and the social atmosphere to seriously network.

DO BUSINESS CARD EXCHANGES REALLY WORK?

Yes!

Because of a continuing group of new participants there seems always to be a divergent enough group to provide viable prospects for those who attend.

The effective exchange of cards in the setting of a structured "exchange" is based on the complete concept of networking. You just begin with the card exchange. From there, you have to – in as short a time as possible – develop a rapport with those people who you perceive to be good additions to your network. Then you should make notes on their business cards (or in a notebook later) so you can add their names to your database.

At this point the networking process continues, using all of the techniques outlined in these chapters.

Author Ken Erdman's son Larry, who is in the environmental clean-up business, attended a card exchange sponsored by the Philadelphia Chamber of Commerce. When he arrived he found the group made up seemingly of people from businesses with no use for his services. By the end of the gathering, however, he had come up with one good prospect and one contact name from an interested company.

Considering the dollar volume involved with a new customer, Larry thought he had a productive "after hours" hour.

On the other hand, Ken's son Dave, a marketing consultant, finds many more leads at these sessions, but also finds more competition among other attendees for his various services.

Like brother Larry, Dave feels that time spent exchanging cards after hours is very productive networking time.

BUSINESS NETWORKING CLUBS

Business networking clubs are much more structured, meeting on a regular (monthly) basis and most often charging membership fees or dues annually or per meeting.

Frequently these clubs meet in the morning, but this early meeting time often rates mixed reviews. The "early birds" feel that they get charged-up and ready to take on the world following a networking session. The "night people" reluctantly accept the sunrise sessions, recognizing that they'll get business by making the 7:00 AM sacrifice.

Some of the clubs are run on a co-op basis but most are run for profit.

The organizers not only provide the meeting place and opportunity for a meal (paid for by the members) but they also impose rules and regulations. Frequently the number of members per chapter is strictly limited. Some clubs admit only one member representing a particular business or profession. Organizers or officers will often make inspection trips to applicants' places of business to make sure that they conform to expected standards.

Some clubs require regular attendance and expect members to regularly exchange leads. Still another possible requirement is that members are expected to give a short program on their product or service – which provides added interest and a member benefit that helps justify fees. In order to stimulate acquaintanceship, some clubs require members to shake hands and or exchange business cards with everyone in attendance. To insure compliance there are secret greeters; if you miss greeting them you are fined.

Membership in the networking club is made up of business and professional people. At meetings you'll find retailers, craftspeople and salespeople for every imaginable product and service. Professionals including doctors, dentists, architects, accountants and lawyers are attracted to networking clubs as a means of getting new clients without overt advertising.

Each member can not only network with the expectation of getting business from fellow members (a big inducement to membership) but they can also expect to get leads from members for prospects outside the club.

If for example, a real estate member has just sold a house, he or she will pass the name of the buyer along to others in the group who have products or services that might be used by the new homeowner.

LE TIP INTERNATIONAL, INC.

LeTip International, Inc. is a California based network of networking clubs typical of the many clubs springing up around the country. LeTip has more than three hundred chapters in Southern California and Arizona and 9,000 members across the United States. It is continually expanding.

Ken Peterson, a life insurance broker, founded LeTip in 1978. He now works full time for the organization. In a recent quote, Peterson said he likes running LeTip International more than selling life insurance. "You help so many people," he said. "I feel like I have helped everyone in the room be more successful in their lives." Ken's no-nonsense approach is designed to really help people network their way to success. Breakfast meetings start promptly at 7:16 AM and end just as promptly at 8:31 AM!

Why join LeTip? Their brochure provides six good reasons, not only for joining LeTip but also for joining a networking club in your area:

- Exchange valuable business tips which turn into $$$$.

- LeTip is an organization of professionals. Professional standards and ethics are maintained by all members in accordance with a set of bylaws.

- LeTip works to provide you with qualified business leads.

- It provides access to clients you would not otherwise be able to contact.

- There are no outside speakers. On a regular basis you will be able to show samples of your work and speak to the members.

- No conflicts of interests are allowed. Your competition can't join once you've joined.

When members were asked at a recent LeTip breakfast, "How many here have made money from last week's tips?" a sea of hands went up.

PROFESSIONAL WOMEN'S NETWORK

Another approach to serious networking is the Professional Women's Network of Honolulu, Hawaii. The group started in 1978 with only six to eight members. Their purpose was to provide mutual support and to exchange business ideas, leads and information.

Interest in the group proved so strong that within six months larger luncheon meetings with speakers were held. The club adopted by-laws, initiated a membership program and had its "official" beginning with 56 charter members. Today there are more than 250 professional women included in the group's membership.

The brochure of the Professional Women's Network describes how the group works:

• **The Network** is a group of dynamic professional women who are actively seeking ways to expand their business position in the Hawaii market place.

• **The Network's Objectives** are to promote the exchange of professional ideas and to provide an opportunity to share experiences of Hawaii's unique market place.

• **Membership** consists of professional business women in Hawaii. New members must attend three luncheons or functions within a six month period before a review by the Board of Directors. New members must be sponsored by a current member in good standing. There is a membership fee.

• **Monthly Meetings** are held to feature outstanding speakers and to provide a regular time and place for the exchange of professional ideas and information.

• **A Network Newsletter** is published monthly and sent to members to provide a communication vehicle for business women in Hawaii and to give notice of the luncheon meetings.

• **A Membership Directory** is provided to each member. This very complete directory includes a brief description of the organization and its aims, listings of officers and past officers, and listings of members, both alphabetically and by types of businesses. Additionally, each member receives a business card sized accordion fold member telephone list.

• **Special Events** are held regularly. These events allow members and guests to meet and get to know each other in a fun and informal setting.

The Professional Women's Network continues to grow each year, providing the women of Hawaii the opportunity for intellectual enrichment and professional enhancement in a business forum.

COMMERCIAL NETWORKS

Commercial networks, developed on a for-profit basis, offer aid to those seeking professional help in a wide variety of fields. These networks put those looking for specific information in touch with individual people who might be of help. Commercial networking groups assess a charge based on online access to their substantial databases.

Teltech, Inc. of Eden Prairie, Minnesota, serves as a typical example. The company was started in the mid '80's by Joe Shuster, an owner of his own small technical business. As an engineer, he would find himself challenged to understand and apply new or emerging technologies or to find an answer to a technical problem.

He would also discover, however, that a source to provide the information he needed was not always within easy reach. "It was like being in a dark room trying to find the light switch," said Shuster. Teltech has not only solved *his* problem. Through the networking process, it's solved a continuing problem for others in need of hard-to-find technical information.

Teltech provides a unique on-line technical information service that matches engineers and scientists in person-to-person contact in more than 1,400 technical areas. The company also provides, by phone and computer, computerized literature searches. Customers have access to more than 5,000 experts who quickly available to provide information or solve problems in many technical areas.

Using their PC's plus software provided by Teltech, subscribers punch in key words to get the names of up to eight authorities in a given field. Experts listed in the database are carefully selected from major American universities, national laboratories, consulting groups and the ranks of top industry retirees. The resource covers virtually every area of science and technology.

PROFESSIONAL NETWORKING GROUPS

Whether you join an informal gathering of interested networkers, a business card exchange, a structured club, or a commercial information exchange group, join up for increased networking success.

23

Spare Time Networking

Networking through sports and hobbies

Probably everyone reading this book participates in some sport or pursues a hobby. Either of these activities opens up a whole new world of networking, an opportunity many may have not considered for active networking.

Hobbies can be classified into two distinct segments – active hobbies, such as raising and showing dogs in competition or passive hobbies such as stamp collecting, which can be followed at home and alone.

Similarly, sports can be divided into two categories, team sports where you interact with a group, or singular sports such as jogging or weight lifting which, again, can be done at home and alone.

DIVERSITY IS THE KEY

In any of the above situations your participation can vary from no networking, to casual networking to active networking. The decision is yours. Serious networkers – those who are reaching for success – should look to their hobby and sport participation as an ideal way to enlarge their networks with a new and diverse group of people.

Frequently the people in your hobby/sports network will be substantially different than those in your business, work, profession or your close friends network. Their economic, social, financial and age differences will not necessarily match yours. But that's a real advantage. It provides you with a window into other lifestyles and personalities. Your networking world will certainly expand in proportion to your active involvement in either sports or hobbies.

SPORTS POSSIBILITIES

As a tennis player, you can have a small group of friends with whom you play on a regular basis – the same friends week after week. Or, in addition to your weekly matches, you can sign up for tennis round-robins, tennis parties or just show up at the courts and let the pro match you up with someone else looking for a partner. In the first instance your networking possibilities are limited. If you follow the other examples you've opened up your potential for enlarging your network.

Even your interest in spectator sports can lead to enlarged networks. Many people who avidly follow a particular sport will join spectator groups or pep clubs that are active both during and in between the sports season.

Have you ever gone to a football tailgating party, or seen one? People seem to become one big family. It could easily be one big *networking* family.

Non-spectator sports have their own special opportunities for expanding networks. Most have clubs or special interest groups which promote the sport and are available to those sports enthusiasts.

If you are an ardent hunter or fisher you can easily find a local hunting and fishing club. Or you may find a local chapter of a hunting or fishing conservation group such as Ducks Unlimited.

Competitions in individual sports are also readily available in varying skill levels. Reading the sports section of your local paper will give you clues to upcoming events.

HOBBIES

A friend of ours is a model train enthusiast. He has many networking opportunities. He could stay at home and work on his trains and show them to friends and neighbors that might stop in. Or he could join a model train club, attend meetings, visit other collectors' homes, attend model train shows and exhibits and go to swap meets (if not to buy, then to meet other train enthusiasts). Look at the variety of networking opportunities.

Dr. Karl Arbogast, of Dallas, Pennsylvania has what we believe to be an unusual hobby. His interest is in lighter-than-air craft... dirigibles or blimps. It's basically a reading and research hobby. The networking possibilities seem limited at best. But Dr. Arbogast expands his network by offering to lecture on the subject to interested groups. He makes his presentation not only interesting but also exciting with intimate stories of such famous ships as the Hindenberg. As a result of knowing of his special interest, people in his new-found network sometimes send him clipping and articles they find about dirigibles.

The same concept might work for you. It's the "try giving your self away" technique. You always seem to get more in return than what you give.

Ray Brandt of Fort Washington, Pennsylvania combines his interest in railroading with travel. He is not only an active member of railroading groups, but he and his wife frequently use their vacation time for unusual railroading trips. They've gone on steam engine junkets, ridden the famed Orient Express and toured much of Europe with a group sponsored by the Overland Chapter of the National Railway Historical Society.

SPARE TIME NETWORKING

Any level of participation in hobbies and sports should provide excitement, fun, discovery, relaxation, physical or mental improvement and satisfaction – or a combination of all of these. With planning and just a little extra effort, you can add networking contacts to the list of benefits.

24

Networking in Your House of Worship

Your extended family

We walk a thin line when we try to adapt a primarily business networking concept to the church, synagogue, shrine or temple. Yet, in a bulletin from a church we visited, there it was: Networking classes, Wednesday night, 7:00 PM.

"So," we said, "why not devote (no pun intended) some space in the book to networking and one's house of worship?"

INTERNAL NETWORKING

For the purposes of this chapter we hope you'll permit us to use the term church to include houses of worship for all religions.

There seem to be several ways networking can be important in the church. In most churches the family concept prevails. The church building serves as the church home for the family. The hope of church leaders is for the congregation, or church family, to get to know each other. But, depending on the size of the congregation, this is not always possible under ordinary circumstances.

At some time before, during or after services we are encouraged to get to know one another through mutual greeting.

Unfortunately these introductions are frequently short-lived. Networking, we believe, can produce more lasting relationships.

How do you network in a church? Easy. Just participate. The more activities in which you are involved, the more people with whom you can network. Churches offer a myriad of opportunities for meeting new friends. Within the church consider the choir, family activities, school or classes, camping, day trips, church suppers, participation on the various organizational committees, decorating committees, the official church boards.

EXTERNAL NETWORKING

The work of the church is not confined to the church building. Just as there are activities within the walls of your house of worship, so too are there opportunities through the work of the church in the community.

Participation in canvassing teams for new members introduces you to your neighbors. Church services and charitable activities put you in touch with still another group of people. Working at fairs and bazaars provides you with people with whom you can network. Let's not forget visiting the sick and elderly. If there is ever a desperate need for networkers it's for those who will do visitations to hospitals, nursing homes and facilities for the aged.

Family networking can be accomplished through participation in church retreats, school activities, camping trips, or special church sponsored trips and tours. For singles, young or old, your church is the ideal place to network for people of like interests – a great starting point for people with either a casual or serious interest in a personal relationship.

RECRUITING IN THE CHURCH

We spotted a typical example of networking in the church in an item appearing in ***INC. Magazine***. The article pointed out that Ronald Sandmeyer, Sr., president of Sandmeyer Steel Company of Philadelphia, was finding it particularly difficult to find people qualified to work in his stainless steel processing plant.

To solve the problem, Sandmeyer turned to a local church. He believed that people with a sense of religion have close family ties and a strong code of ethics.

His theory proved right. Since he started recruiting from local churches he has had excellent results. He now has three churches in his network. "The ministers do the screening for me. They don't send loafers or drifters, just solid citizens," he said.

Increasingly, people looking for jobs, or employers looking for help, turn to church networking.

YOUR EXTENDED FAMILY

Of all the networking possibilities we write of in this book, church networking probably provides the greatest opportunity to make the greatest number of and longest lasting friendships. You now have an extended family – your church family.

The unique part about church networking is that in your efforts to expand your network through active participation you are giving of yourself to your God's work. What a wonderful bonus!

25

Giving Yourself Away

Volunteer networking

Perhaps your most rewarding networking will be done in volunteer groups or when you are doing volunteer work.

Volunteering and networking are made for each other. They bring together a combination of wants and needs and they offer a combination of giving and receiving of talents and joys. Anybody who has actively pursued any kind of volunteer effort will, we're sure, tell of the satisfaction, many personal joys and spiritual enrichment of helping someone in need.

Volunteering is growing in the United States. A Gallup Poll of 1990 showed that charitable giving had grown substantially from 1987 to 1989. The study also reported large increases in church attendance. And more and more people are becoming involved in volunteering. It's been estimated that over ninety-eight million men, women and children are involved in volunteer work. These volunteers cross all age, ethnic and income groups. We are fast becoming a nation of volunteers.

THE NEED FOR VOLUNTEERS

Today, perhaps more than at any time in our country's history, we have a critical need for volunteers. Our news headlines seem to daily scream of drug related crimes, deaths by drugs, alcohol related auto accidents and the plight of the homeless. We're fast becoming a nation of elderly people – people who, in many cases, can't completely help themselves. Increasing unemployment and broken marriages result in further problems that can be helped through volunteering.

It would not be difficult for any networker to find a place to use time, talent, skills or money to alleviate some measure of human distress.

GIVING YOUR SELF AWAY

In an earlier chapter we mention David Dunn's wonderful book, ***Try Giving Yourself Away.*** In his book Dunn suggests, "Each of us gets an allotment of time – twenty four hours each day of the year. Even the busiest of us has from a few minutes to an hour or more a day which we could give others in the form of some useful service." He continues, "In terms of downright happiness, it is my experience that returns-per-minute from *giving* are far greater than the returns from *getting*."

We continue to emphasize that networking should not be a selfish pursuit. To truly work, networking must involve both giving and receiving.

Wally "Famous" Amos, who so kindly wrote the introduction to this book, said it aptly: "Lead a life of service to your fellow human beings, giving your all to that purpose, and you will have nothing else in life to worry about."

THE OPPORTUNITIES FOR VOLUNTEERING

Opportunities for volunteering (and volunteer networking) abound. Even a casual reading of your daily paper or a few minutes in front of the evening television news should provide sufficient ideas for putting your "service" time to use.

Volunteering can be done both through individual involvement or through organized volunteer and charitable groups. You can present yourself directly to those who need help, such as contacting a local nursing home and offering your services. You can participate in the volunteer efforts of a group such as your church, a service club or a volunteer group dedicated to a particular cause.

NETWORKING ASPECTS OF VOLUNTEERING

Volunteering opens wide the doors for every form of networking. The opportunity is provided for social, business and professional networking. You'll meet new friends and work together side by side with fellow business and professional people. The "working together for a worthy common cause" aspect will create strong personal ties.

Your volunteer networking process will employ all of the tactics you use for other forms of networking. You will be creating a data base of those you work with and for, writing letters and notes, making telephone calls, attending social and charitable affairs, perhaps working on a newsletter, asking for help and, frequently, saying "thank you."

TREVOR'S CAMPAIGN FOR THE HOMELESS

Sometimes, the volunteer work done by the individual grows to proportions beyond the ability and energy for the person that started the work. This is how many charitable organizations get started. A networking story that quickly comes to mind is Trevor's Campaign for the Homeless.

Trevor Ferrell, in 1983 at age 11, saw the plight of the homeless in Philadelphia while watching a local news broadcast. That night, Trevor convinced his parents, Janet and Frank, to sacrifice a comfortable night at home and take him into center city Philadelphia. That first night he gave his own extra blanket and pillow to the first "street person" he met.

With networking and the support of his family, classmates and friends, Trevor began to make nightly trips into Philadelphia to distribute the food, clothing and blankets that he and others had collected.

Within two years after Trevor's Campaign began, Trevor and his family had networked over a thousand volunteers to help cook and deliver hot meals nightly to the homeless. Also, a 33 room boarding house was donated to Trevor to help his mission. It is known simply as Trevor's Place and houses up to 40 homeless people. Trevor's Next Door is a home for homeless women and their children.

Trevor's original act of kindness and charity has grown to seventeen chapters, with the latest opened in Paris, France. Trevor's father, Frank, is president of the non-profit corporation and his mother, Janet, is vice-president. The Trevor's Campaign National Advisory Board contains such famous names as: Pat Boone, Helen Hayes, Dr. C. Everett Koop and Dr. Robert Schuller.

THE REWARDS OF VOLUNTEERING

Your personal rewards for volunteering won't necessarily come easily. Volunteering requires time, work, patience, endurance, stamina, understanding, and sometimes even enduring a lack of appreciation. But the rewards are worth every bit of anything you sacrifice for your particular cause.

The rewards include the appreciation of your work, the sense of joy that comes from seeing the good you have done, the admiration of your peers, the opportunity to network with an entirely different group of people and the opportunity to make new and lasting friendships.

An interesting reward for volunteering is documented in a study done by the University of Michigan Survey Research center. They followed 2,700 people over a ten year period to determine the impact of social relationships on health. They found that regular volunteer work, more than any other social activity, dramatically increased life expectancy! Now that's a really great reward.

See the Toolbox section at the end of the book for a directory of service organizations.

26

Putting It All Together

Networking and selling

Networking to sell a product or service is probably the most recognized and most often used form of this specialized communications process.

Aside from the product or services sold, networking is a selling process in many of its other applications. When you are socially networking, networking for a new job or networking to advance in your company, you're really selling yourself.

For suggestions on networking techniques that will help you sell, whatever your product or service, just go back through the book. Previous chapters explain in detail how to network and what tools to use for most selling situations. There are, however some situations in sales that require specific networking techniques.

SPECIAL SELLING SITUATIONS

Several well known areas of sales that we feel are especially suited to networking include: real estate, insurance, automobiles, investments, office equipment (fax machines, copiers, etc.), cellular phones and the whole range of products promoted through direct selling (more about this later).

LEADS AND REFERRALS

Many salespeople lump leads and referrals together and call them prospects. There's a big difference between a lead and a referral. A lead can come from someone answering an ad in a trade magazine or looking you up in the phone book. A lead is very important, but it's a name without a reference or connection. You can get plenty of leads without networking. (But, with networking, you can get even *more* leads.)

Referrals from networking sources are more vital. They come from someone who has pre-introduced you and has recommended you. The personal referral is the highest level of networking for sales.

THE REAL ESTATE EXAMPLE

To get a personal opinion of the importance of networking for referrals, we asked veteran real estate salesman Larry Nehasil of RE/MAX Crossroads, in Minnesota to comment on how he feels about referrals:

"Referrals are the lifeblood of the Professional Realtor. No other form of sales lead can equal the personal referral for quality and rate of conversion to an absolute sale. Referrals usually carry a personal recommendation that is highly accepted by the prospective client and provides an excellent 'door opener' for the Real Estate Profession."

Larry continues, "The efficient use and management of a seller's time will determine the degree of success a Realtor will have in the market place. A very well organized weekly schedule must include the establishment, operation and maintenance of a referral network system. Without a referral network system, a sufficient level of active prospects cannot be maintained to assure an adequate number of appointments."

Larry's comments, we think, apply appropriately to the other forms of selling mentioned earlier in this chapter.

NETWORK MARKETING (MULTILEVEL MARKETING)

Starting as early as the 1700's when "Yankee peddlers" went from town to town selling their wares from saddle bags, networking has played an important role in *direct sales,* those sales made on a one-to-one basis – no middle person involved.

In this century people such as Alfred Fuller, H. J. Heinz and William Wrigley started with direct selling and went on to build huge business empires. Networking figured prominently, even in those early days. As customers told their friends and the friends told other friends, a *network* of buyers developed.

Today, this earliest form of direct selling has been refined still further. In a sales system popularly referred to as Network Sales or Multilevel Marketing or just MLM, the person-to-person concept has been expanded and refined.

HOW NETWORK/MULTILEVEL MARKETING WORKS

In multilevel marketing the seller is no longer a door-to-door salesperson. Rather he or she becomes a distributor (without a store) selling to the people they know. As they expand, they develop a second tier of salespeople selling the same products to a new and different audience. The second tier can now establish yet another tier, with each higher tier participating in the profits through commissions and overriding bonuses of its next lower tier.

Profits are increased for all participants, as the cost of middle people such as wholesalers, retailers, and jobbers are eliminated. The basis of this unique concept is that the original multilevel marketer is self-replicating, self-financed and self-motivated.

THE INTEGRITY OF THE SYSTEM

It's important to recognize that in multilevel marketing, salespeople need only to sell product. This is very much unlike the widely publicized pyramid schemes and scams of the past where distributors had to make large payments of money to the sales company.

WELL KNOWN NETWORK MARKETERS

Some names of widely recognized multilevel marketing companies include:

Amway Corporation
Avon Products
Discovery Toys
Ecko Home Products Company
Electrolux Corporation
Encyclopedia Britannica, Inc.
The Fuller Brush Company
The Hanover Shoe Company
Highlights For Children, Inc.
The Kirby Company
Mary Kay Cosmetics, Inc.
Nu-Skin International, Inc.
Regal Ware, Inc.
Salad Master, Inc.
Shaklee Corporation
Time-Life Books, Inc.
The West Bend Company
World Book, Inc.

NETWORKING FOR NETWORK SELLING

Mark Moroney, a long-time network marketer from Minnesota, credits networking with his selling success. In seven short months as a Shaklee distributor he and his wife Gayle earned a bonus car and a trip to Shaklee's San Francisco headquarters. He comments, "In order to become successful in network marketing in a short period of time you need to not just work hard, but you need to work smart. This is where networking comes into play."

He further suggests that to find other people who want to start their own distributorships under you, join or start a networking organization. "What you're looking for," he says, "is a person with a desire for their own business and the proper timing for them to act upon this desire."

Mark's keys to a successful network marketing plan are:

1) Have a unique, top quality product line that will gain a loyal customer base.

2) The product line should be consumable and will be reordered.

3) The company should offer ample rewards and income to motivate the independent.

4) The company must have integrity and financial strength to last into the future.

THE FUTURE OF NETWORK MARKETING

The *Wall Street Journal* predicts that in the 1990's more than 50% of services and goods sold in the United States will be sold through network/multilevel channels. Major corporations such as MCI and US Sprint have used MLM sales forces. Other major corporations, eager to reach prospects on a face-to-face basis, are rapidly embracing a concept based on good old networking principals

LIFE IS A SELLING NETWORK

Our friend Mark Moroney, said it so well: " Life is a network. My favorite come-back to the individual who says, 'I can't sell,' is, 'Your whole life is selling.' As a child, you sold your mother on when to feed you. You sold your teacher on the idea that you were a good student. You sold your spouse on the idea that they should marry you, and you'll probably sell the boss on letting you keep your job or giving you a raise."

Success Stories

People Who Have Networked Their Way to Success

A Selection of Case Histories

Success
Story #1

The Million Dollar Haircut

Learning by networking

Joe Francis, Sr.
Chairman of the Board
The Barbers, Hairstyling for Men & Women, Inc.
Minneapolis, Minnesota

Joe Francis started out in 1962 cutting men's hair for $1.75 a cut. Today he operates over 500 hair salons called "Cost Cutters" and "City Looks."

How did he network his way to success? Let Joe tell you himself.

JOE'S STORY

One of the most effective ways to learn new things, to explore new ideas or to meet new and exciting people is through networking. Networking is nothing more than getting out there and putting yourself in front of someone. You can do it in person, by letter or telephone.

When I first started in the barbering business, the average national price of a haircut varied from shop to shop by only about a quarter – between $1.50 and $1.75. Your income was determined by how many heads you could cut in one day. The average shop was a "one chair" business with maybe a helper for the busy times.

I had a "two-chair" shop, and I worked hard to keep the chairs filled. After six years in the business with this set-up, though, I began to feel locked in. I could cut only so many heads and charge only so much; prices were pretty much fixed. I asked myself, "Is this the way I want to spend the rest of my career?"

Luckily, about this time, I came across an article in a national magazine about a barber in Hollywood who was charging $25.00 for a hair cut! Wow! He had made a name for himself as a "hair stylist to the stars."

Who is this guy? How can he get away with that? More importantly, how can *I* do that? I had to meet him.

Soon I was in California in the shop of the twenty five dollar stylist. I wanted desperately to find out what he knew that I didn't know. Fortunately he was very approachable, very proud of what he did and eager to share his successful concept. He told me of how he introduced hair styling as an opportunity to break away from the traditional haircut and give the customer special attention and a new look. He had also upgraded his shop, which appealed to a higher income clientele.

I certainly couldn't get way with a $25.00 cut in St. Paul, Minnesota, but I could offer something different – hair styling, and a new shop in a new neighborhood.

First I learned to do the European Razor Cut. It was a popular styling process in Europe but new to the United States. After two years of learning the new styling technique I opened the fanciest barber shop in the Twin Cities, in one of the highest retail rental areas. I charged, not $25.00, but $5.75 – and still my fellow barbers were amazed at my price.

And my customers were amazed at how good they looked after a razor cut style. My new concept worked! People were more than satisfied and, best of all, they didn't object to the price.

As news of my shop spread by word of mouth, my wife called the local newspaper and they came to see the shop. They did a feature article on the new *six chair hair styling salon.* I had *six* barbers working, all of whom I had trained to do razor cut styling.

The rest is history.

NETWORKING COMES TO THE RESCUE...AGAIN

Joe's shop quickly grew into five shops and eventually he again felt the need for a new challenge. In 1968 he decided he ought to franchise his shops but he knew nothing about franchising. Remembering the results of networking with the California stylist, Joe realized he again had to network with someone who could help him.

A magazine article Joe read mentioned the International Franchise Association. He joined, met the people who were both emerging franchise owners and those who were eminently successful, and learned about franchising. At the association's conventions he met such people as Bill Rosenberg, the founder of Dunkin' Donuts, and Art Bartlett, the founder of Century Twenty One.

A 500 SHOP FRANCHISE COMPANY

Joe learned well, and he created the first National Barbershops Franchise. Today his company franchises over 500 shops across the United States. He now serves as a member of the Board of Directors of the International Franchise Association.

"Now I have a chance to share with others my experience just as others have done for me. Networking is a two-way street," he says. "You have to give as well as receive."

POLITICAL NETWORKING

Some years ago Joe discovered that his local Senator was going to vote *against* post secondary education funding, which would cut off funds to barber school students, among others. Joe had to change his mind!

He decided that the best approach was networking – to get "in front" of the Senator. Luck was with him when he learned that the Senator would be one of the speakers at a luncheon sponsored by the local Chamber of Commerce. Each speaker was assigned a table, and Joe arranged to get there early and to sit at the Senator's table. As luck again would have it, the Senator sat next to Joe.

Joe introduced himself simply as, "Joe, the barber."

In the ensuing conversation, the Senator mentioned that he badly needed a haircut for an important engagement that night...could Joe take care of him?

You bet!

"Although I personally hadn't cut hair for almost twenty years, I had a plan," Joe said. "I would let him think he was coming to my shop, but, instead I would take him to my corporate headquarters. Our training director would give him his hair cut, and while he was confined under a drape, I would have a captive audience to listen to my views on the post secondary education funding bill."

Joe got his point across to the much surprised Senator. Interestingly, the Senator was himself a franchiser in the plywood industry. This combination of circumstances led to a genuine interest in Joe's views. The Senator became an ally and was very instrumental in helping Joe's industry.

"I've had many more networking successes both here in the United States and in countries around the world," Joe says. "When properly approached, people are willing to help you and to share their experiences. All you have to do is ask. That's what networking is all about."

Joe Francis, Sr. was recently selected by national sponsors Ernst & Young, Merrill Lynch and ***INC. Magazine*** *as 1990 Minnesota Entrepreneur of the Year. Local sponsorship included the law firm of Gray, Plant, Mooty, Mooty and Bennett, PA.*

Success Story #2

Doggone Good Networking

Turning hobbies to profit

Judi Carson
Breeder, Trainer, Exhibitor of Pure Breed Dogs, American Kennel Club Show Champions and Obedience Title Holders
Co-owner, Canine Shenanigans

My hobby is raising and training show dogs. Several years ago, Rae Tanner, a woman I knew only casually from a dog training class, called me with an idea she had for a new business. "You have great contacts in the dog world," she said. "Maybe we can get together and make some extra money."

Her idea was to develop a logo for a new dog hobby called "Agility", a sport brought over from England and quickly becoming very popular in this country. Agility is running dogs through an obstacle course against the clock.

Rae and I each invested $500.00. We contacted an artist to refine our logo idea and to turn it into printable art. We decided that our products would be T-shirts, sweat shirts, magnets, bumper stickers, note tablets, dog bone shaped pencils and a few other "doggie things."

The unique part of our relationship, and the reason my new partner came to me, is that my full time job involves selling imprinted advertising specialties (like T-shirts, magnets and bumper stickers). I was in the right business and had the right contacts to produce our "Agility" products and turn our ideas to dollars.

My first step was to go to my employer and tell him about our idea and my plans for participating part-time and at home in this new hobby-related business. I knew that without his full knowledge and full support the concept would never work nor be as successful as it has been. I've never been shy about turning to my network for help. In this case, if I became successful, my boss's business would benefit since I would buy my products through his company.

We started out selling at our own local dog club's Agility workshops. We did so well that we turned to selling at as many other workshops and competitions as we could find, traveling hundreds of miles in each direction from home. Our ultimate goal was to get to England to see and sell at the English Agility events at the Cruft's Dog Show, a 4 day show with more than 25,000 dogs competing (the most prestigious dog event in the world).

As we grew, we started advertising on a monthly basis in a national Dog Obedience newspaper. Through this advertising exposure and my networking contacts with dog show people it became known that I could also imprint other products or the same products personalized with a dog club's name. Many of these products could be used as judge's gifts or prizes for competitions. Additionally, I always let people know that I was in the imprinted advertising specialty business and could provide imprinted give-aways for their business or hobbies.

I had the best of both worlds. I networked my hobby contacts for my job and my hobby business provided revenue for the company I worked for.

As my friends assumed more and more responsibilities within their clubs and were more involved with the organization of events , they thought of me. They may not have known what I did in "real life," but they associate me with selling T-shirts and other Agility imprinted products at shows. They would often tell their national or regional breed show committees that "they knew someone in the business" that could get them trophies, judge's gifts or hand-outs for up-coming shows.

Because I am a "dog show person" I understand the process of dog club boards and budgets. Since show committees are often spread out throughout the country, it sometimes takes a long time for a club to choose which imprinted items it wants to use to represent its event. Approvals of products and designs take time (sometimes up to a year). Clubs plan their shows up to 3 or 4 years ahead of time. I usually get actively involved about 18 months before the show date.

My reputation as "a dog show person" gave me credibility in my networking. In selling conversations, I had all of the right questions to ask and I could take a personal interest in other peoples' dogs and dog show trials and tribulations. People tended to take a "let's keep it in the family" attitude – they took their business to someone in *their* network.

As people returned from different dog club functions they showed their fellow hobbyists our products which they had received at the regional or national shows. Often they or their friends would then call me. From year to year, as the job of organizing a show was passed from one person to another, my name was passed along, too. My network grew as a result of unique products, good service and reputation. It seemed that for every breed of dog there was a potential dog club to sell to.

The real proof of success for my part of the business was when, having worked with different people on dog show events, they came to me to supply imprinted items or corporate gifts for their businesses. When they call me for *those* items I know that I have made a real customer. All of the networking and doggie talk has paid of in a financially meaningful way.

And the weekend t-shirt business? It's been successful, too. Remember, our goal was to take a trip to England to see the English Agility events at the Cruft's Dog Show. Within two years we had enough profits to send us on our way to jolly old

England. While there, we sold all of the products we brought with us to the National Agility Workshop and brought orders back to be filled when we reached home. What a thrill!

Today, the network has spread and the business continues to grow. Rae recently moved to Chicago, and the partnership flourishes both there and here in the Philadelphia area. Rae and I each need to find someone new now to travel to dog shows with, but we will still go to England again together.

It all started with a casual friend and a phone call...and networking with a fellow hobbyist. The results are a new, fun business for the two of us, more sales for my company's products, and a substantially enhanced friendship.

Perhaps the best part of my hobby networking is that it's not one-sided. Occasionally my full-time business clients are looking for dogs and call me for advice or call to ask questions about training or breeding.

I not only sell, but I can help my networking contacts in a very personal way.

Success Story #3

Bald Networking

Making something out of nothing

John T. Capps, III
Founder and Executive Director
Bald Headed Men of America
102 Bald Drive
Morehead City, North Carolina

Networking was not even a word in our marketing vocabulary when John T. Capps, III founded the Bald Headed Men of America in 1972.

The concept of bald friends knowing other bald friends was the basis of what is now a worldwide network of proud bald headed men (and women). These networkers believe that what's in the head is more important than what's on top of it – or not on top of it.

John turned bald at a very early age. At 15 he was already on his way to a hair-free life. He suffered the same ridicule and jokes as his older counterparts. Several years later, just out of college, he was turned down for a job by a large Atlanta financial institution. Capps was told that the company was looking for a "youthful, dynamic personality." As a bald headed man, even one just out of school, John didn't fit that mold.

At the age of thirty, he decided not to cover up with a hairpiece, to cease denying and apologizing, and to simply live with his shining bald head. He made another very important decision. He not only would accept his baldness, but he would laugh about it – and get other "baldies" to do the same. John figured that the inferiority complex caused by baldness might be overcome with a little humor.

"Might as well," said John, who is also president of a quick-printing and public relations company, "because humor is probably the only thing that will help."

THE BALD HEADED MEN OF AMERICA

With the decision to turn to humor as the true remedy for baldness, John came up with what seemed like a crazy idea – to start a club for bald headed men. After all, what's wrong with being bald? The Lord made millions and millions of heads – those He was ashamed of, He covered up! John Capps would meet the problem of baldness "head on."

He started Bald Headed Men of America (BHMA).

Membership in his elite group was limited to those who have a bald spot, chrome dome, or haircut with a noticeable hole in it. Members pay a $10.00 initiation fee and $10.00 a year dues. They receive a handsome certificate attesting to both their baldness and their membership in an organization that doesn't "go around fooling mother nature."

The "baldies" are more than just a fun group. They are also a serious self-help organization with a mission to help those for whom baldness creates psychological problems.

NETWORKING SOMETHING FROM NOTHING

As a third generation baldy, John first wrote to his bald dad, his bald uncles, bald friends and others of hairless recognition. Where did these friends come from? Networking! John had kept business cards and noted "bald" on the back of the cards from other baldies. For several years, he had maintained a list of bald Rotary club members, bald Jaycees, and some bald church and business contacts. It was his bald database.

Once the BHMA was started and the initial invitations for membership were received, the new members were sent sheets and asked to fill in the names of other prospects so information could be sent to them. This networking system is still used today.

The network of bald people knowing other bald people in all walks of life began to grow and the BHMA has been growing ever since...because of lack of growth. John truly networked nothing (a lack of hair) into something (BHMA), his bald headed organization.

P.R. – THE BALD FACTS

As a P.R. person, John recognized that the media would play an important role in sharing both the fun and the seriousness of his organization. He started networking media contacts.

Doug Looney, a writer for the ***National Observer*** weekly newspaper and now a writer for ***Sports Illustrated,*** became interested in BHMA. His bald story appeared on a front page of the ***National Observer*** with photographs. A friend of Doug's from ***Time*** magazine networked with him and did a bald story for ***Time*** in their health section

Jules Loh, special events writer for the Associated Press in New York City, noted the ***Time*** story and made a visit to Morehead City, North Carolina to see first hand if the BHMA was for real. Jules' respect, coupled with the extensive network of the Associated Press, provided additional exposure in hundreds of newspapers worldwide for John's now-growing-famous organization.

From that article, individual news organizations had their own writers do independent stories on Bald Headed Men of America. Andrea Higbee, writer for the ***New York Times,*** vacationed near Morehead City and discovered for herself the amazing club for baldies. She later did a feature on the club that appeared in her paper

John's networking really works. He's taken advantage of every networking tool available including newsletters, direct mail, the telephone and of course, public relations.

His results have averaged three radio interviews each week, two televisions interviews per month, five requests for bald material and information from freelance writers per week and one magazine news story per month for the past several years.

THE BOOK ON BALDNESS

Author Richard Sandomir of New York came across the BHMA while researching his book ***Bald Like Me***. About the same time, Dennis Kelley of the ***New York Daily News*** published a story on the BHMA. Two New York writers writing about baldness!

As part of his research, Richard Sandomir contacted the BHMA for information about the club. He attended the annual Bald Headed Men Of America Convention two years in a row. (The convention is held the second weekend of September in the Bald-room of the Holiday Inn in Morehead City.) With his personal knowledge of the BHMA organization, Richard completed his book (published by the McMillan Company). He subsequently did the talk show circuit it and, through networking with other baldies of the BHMA, appeared on various shows including the *Sally Jessy Raphael Show.*

NETWORKING FOR TV COVERAGE

Networking has been good to the Bald Headed Men of America. Through continual contact with media people, John Capps has appeared on such prominent shows as: *Donahue, Good Morning America, This Morning On CBS, The Today Show, Night Line, CBS Evening News with Dan Rather, Hour Magazine,* PBS's *Nova* television series, *Real People, What's My Line, I've Got A Secret* and *20/20*.

Not bad for someone who couldn't get a job because he was bald!

Other baldies like CBS's Harry Smith and NBC's Willard Scott and Joe Garagiola are willing promoters of baldies. They frequently mention the fun that members of The Bald Headed Men of America have whenever they put their bald heads together in a smooth network.

A NETWORKING SECRET

When asked how networking has helped build the Bald Headed Men of America to a membership of 20,000, John will rub his shiny bald head and say, "Always responding to individual requests from any and everyone who writes. You never know who knows who and who you'll someday need to know. After all, that's what networking is all about."

IT'S NOT ALL JUST FOR FUN

Each year at their convention the baldies take time out from fun and address a serious concern – alopecia areata, a condition that causes loss of hair from *all* parts of the body. Proceeds from the convention and from individual contributions have been allocated to the Alopecia Areata Research Foundation, a group of doctors working to find a cure.

John Capps' unselfish efforts have made many people proud of their "chrome domes." Through humor, John has helped these same people achieve a sense of dignity about their baldness.

Success
Story #4

Show Business

Trade show adventures

Joyce Werkman
President
Instruments For Research and Industry, I²R
Cheltenham, PA

For most who participate in trade shows, the experience is one of fulfilling strictly a sales function – show the products, sell the customer.

For astute networkers a trade show can become even more meaningful. In addition to offering the opportunity of meeting and selling customers and prospects, the trade show offers the people "working" the show the opportunity to network with the other exhibitors – including competitors.

There is also the opportunity to network with people at your booth that may not be customers for your products but who could be valuable contacts in other areas.

As we mentioned in a previous chapter, attending any trade show that particularly relates to your business or profession offers unending possibilities for networking.

As we thought about people who seemed to take maximum advantage of networking at trade shows, the president of a highly successful scientific instrument company came to mind.

It was a Thanksgiving day when a phone call started Joyce Werkman on the road to the presidency of Instruments for Research and Industry, I^2R, a manufacturer of propriatory products for research chemists.

She had placed a situation wanted ad in the local weekly newspaper. In her ad, Joyce mentioned that she was looking for temporary, part-time work. She spelled out when she was available to work and everything she had done. Dan Conlon, then owner of I^2R, read the ad on Thanksgiving morning and decided to call that very day. "Why wait?" he thought. "Chances are she'll be home on the holiday."

Joyce was home. She accepted the job offer and started working for Conlon at I^2R on a new product project. She would be involved in both the manufacturing and shipping of the product.

One of the provisions of the job offer, however, was the success of the product. If it caught on, Joyce could have a permanent job. If it failed, she was out of work. To insure success, Joyce took her work home and spent evenings preparing mailings announcing the new product. She was determined to make sure it was successful. And it *was* successful. The company then added trade shows, in addition to direct mail, to promote and get wide recognition of her product in the trade. Soon her company's Glove Bag was widely accepted in the scientific community.

We asked Joyce Werkman to share a few experiences about her networking adventures at trade shows to include in our book.

Networking at trade shows for I^2R is extremely important. As mentioned before, the company manufactures devices for the research chemist; the products are sold primarily through direct mail. I^2R does not have reps, dealers or salespeople. Their only contact with their customers on a personal basis is at the shows.

I^2R networks at trade shows for a variety of purposes:

- To establish that they are in fact a real entity.
- To give prospective customers a chance to see and handle their products (often in actual operation).
- To provide an opportunity to try out product ideas on customers and prospects (market research).
- As a forum for introducing new products.
- To provide the opportunity to get feedback (both good and bad) for their products and services.

NEW PRODUCTS AND IDEA GENERATION

Aside from using trade shows for these reasons, I^2R enjoys two other major networking benefits from participation in shows.

The first is that they are always on the lookout for new products. Since I^2R does not have salespeople visiting labs, the company misses an opportunity for customer feedback regarding suggestions for new products or changes in current products. Trade shows offer I^2R the opportunity for encounters with customers who want to come to them and say "Why don't you guys make...?" or, "Know what we need...?" This is how many of their new products come into being.

Secondly, I^2R publishes a cartoon calendar which depicts humorous situations in the lab. Since the calendar is an in-house effort, they need all the suggestions they can get for situations to be drawn along with as much critical review and input as their visitors to the booth will give them. The networking contacts that they make at the shows are great for this project.

NETWORKING WITH EXHIBITORS

An exciting opportunity came Joyce's way as a result of trade show networking. She was given the chance to take a leave of absence from I^2R to go to England and work for another company for a short time.

It all started at a show in Sweden at the US Department of Commerce Trade Center. All of the companies exhibiting were

American, and each stand or booth had an American representative in it. It took a couple of days before Joyce was able to convince some of these people that she, too, was American. (Being blonde and tall, Joyce looked more Swedish than American.)

After getting over this hurdle, it was possible to have meaningful conversations with the other exhibitors as to what I^2R is about and what the company's purposes and expectations were regarding this particular show.

As a result of one of those conversations, Joyce was invited to dinner by the two men who were in the booth next to her. They were the corporate head and the international marketing manager of that particular company. It turned out that the corporate head, Doc, was from New Jersey and that the international marketing manager, Frank, was an Austrian now living in Paris.

At some point during the week, Joyce had also met a young Frenchman, Pierre, whose father was the French distributor for this company. Pierre and Joyce held several conversations together: Pierre was anxious to practice his English and he wasn't going to leave any stone unturned in his quest to find a way to get a job in the US (and a Mustang).

Later, Joyce bumped into him again, in the airport in Copenhagen, and he again expressed his desire to find a way to come to the US to work.

After Joyce got home, she thought more about Pierre's wish and finally decided to write a letter to Doc and see if there was any way I^2R could help. Being a small company probably allowed I^2R a lot more flexibility than a large corporation would have in this situation.

Doc responded to Joyce's letter with an invitation to dinner to discuss the situation. In the end, Pierre went to England to work and finally to Canada. For Joyce, however, this was just the beginning. She ended up going to England to work for a summer. She learned a great deal and even got to be responsible for setting up a show for Doc's company in Wales.

What Joyce learned from doing a market research project for Doc's company and setting up the trade show was invaluable experience for both her and I^2R when she returned home.

A REUNION

The adventure continues. A couple of years later, while Joyce was doing a major show in Cleveland, she looked down the aisle and saw her old friends Doc and Frank coming toward her booth. They had called the I^2R office and learned that Joyce was not around. They figured she might have come to Cleveland to the show – and so here they were. They got together for a reunion lunch.

While at lunch Joyce learned that Frank had a sixteen-year-old daughter who wanted to come to the US for a summer of work and an opportunity to improve her English. Anne Lise had been to camp in England for several summers and so did know a fair amount of our language. Anne Lise came, lived with Joyce and worked for I^2R for two summers. After University in France, Anne Lise spent a year teaching English and French at a New England college.

NETWORKING AROUND THE WORLD

From all of these contacts, initiated through networking from her original contact in Sweden, Joyce became a partner in a new company which was started in the United States and connected to a major Swiss precision screw machine parts manufacturer.

Just imagine, from one show, one contact in Sweden – and networking – Joyce ended up with all of these exciting experiences plus good business contacts in England, France, Switzerland and Germany.

For Joyce, networking is what trade shows are all about.

Success Story #5

Mile High Networking

Networking and travel

Willmon White,
Editor
***The Rotarian* Magazine,**
a publication of Rotary International,
Evanston, IL

Travel – especially international travel – always presents opportunities for networking.

Will White is editor of the official magazine of Rotary International and manager of its Communications and Public Relations Division in Evanston, Illinois. He's a strong believer in what he calls *travel networking*. His twenty year career with Rotary has taken him on photo-journalism and public speaking trips to more than twenty nations. Whether in the air or on the ground he's constantly networking with the people he meets.

"It's so easy to add something extra to your trip," he says. "You just have to speak up and show an interest in everyone you meet."

THE INDIA CONNECTION

In October, 1987 Will was covering a meeting of 10,000 Asian Rotarians in Delhi, India. There he met Jan Percival, a Rotarian from San Diego, California. "She was one of only a handful of Westerners at the meeting," says Will.

He continues the story: "I had to find out why she was there...to hear her story. I took Jan's picture and learned that she was a new Rotarian who, almost on a whim, had come to India. She'd visited India once before and decided to take a few weeks off from her public relations business to attend the Asia Rotary conference.

Jan contacted a Rotary governor in India and was able to link up – network style – with a group of Rotary Youth Exchange students who were traveling about in northern India with their adult leaders. Jan, who is 35, slept in the same dorms, ate the same food, and searched for the same elusive roll of toilet paper.

"I asked Jan if she might like to involve her club in a Rotary International service project and got an enthusiastic *yes*! I introduced her to Rajendra K. Saboo, a prominent Rotarian leader who, as is turns out, was Rotary's world president in 1991-92.

"Mr. Saboo is from Chandigarh, India, where there is a world famous rock garden of some 50 acres created entirely from junk – wire, broken stones, glass, and other trash. It's the creation of one determined man with a dream. His name is Nek Chand, and his garden is now considered one of India's national treasures.

AN INTERNATIONAL PROJECT

"Jan and I developed the idea of her Rotary club back home sending a young art student to study as an apprentice under the great master...to learn about found art or junk sculpture...and to also learn about the culture and language of the Indian people. Jan and her club carefully screened applicants and selected Chris Cannestra, a 21-year-old senior at San Diego State University. The Rotarians bought a plane ticket for Chris and sponsored her three-month apprenticeship. In India she stayed in the homes of Chandigarh Rotarians. The hospitality of Indian Rotarians is known to be superb.

"For Chris, it was a life-changing experience. She was a good ambassador for Rotary International and for her sponsoring Rotary club in San Diego. My magazine, ***The Rotarian***, got an unusual story about an international Youth Exchange project. And now, Jan hopes to bring Nek Chand to San Diego with some of his unusual sculpture pieces for an exhibit and demonstration. She is looking for ways to create a Junk Sculpture outdoor park in the San Diego area. Her big dream is to transplant the fantasy rock garden idea to the rich western world which is overflowing – unfortunately – with new material for junk sculpture. The goal: 'beauty from ugliness'."

MILE-HIGH NETWORKING

Editor White's story is one small example of what can happen when one travels and is alert to networking opportunities. As he reports, "Even on the plane, at 35,000 feet, ideas start to spark. Almost invariably, I find something in common with the person in the next seat. There's something invigorating and mind-opening about travel – a kind of magical energy, or synergistic effect, that happens. Serendipity seems the rule rather than the exception. I'm motivated to network to help Rotary's projects and our magazine. And it increases my enjoyment of my work and travel. Simple sight-seeing, in other words, is not enough. Networking adds an extra dimension that I find fun, productive and satisfying."

Success
Story #6

The "Good Old *Girls*" Network

From educator to entrepreneur

Cynthia A. Hudson
Founder and President,
The Waterfront Corporations
A marine construction and commercial diving company
Camden, New Jersey

One of the earliest forms of networking was the "good old boys" network, characterized by a well-to-do gentleman sitting in a leather covered chair in the library of his private club, smoking a cigar and reading the ***Wall Street Journal***.

The "good old boys" traded business favors and influence. It was an "I'll scratch your back if you scratch mine" arrangement.

ENTER THE WOMEN

All of that has changed. At last, women have penetrated the bastions of the formerly all-male clubs and organizations. The typical scene in most private clubs today is likely to be that of a female corporate president entertaining guests in the club's dining room.

Women have at last taken their rightful and much deserved place along side of their male counterparts.

CYNTHIA HUDSON, ENTREPRENEUR

Cindy Hudson moved from being an educator to being an entrepreneur. She founded a marine construction and diving company that operates along Philadelphia's waterfront.

Her credentials include a degree from Albright College in Pennsylvania and a certificate in Construction Management from Drexel University in Philadelphia.

To really get to know her business, Cindy served a three year apprenticeship as a journeyman wharf and dock builder. She is currently a member of the United Brotherhood of Carpenters and Joiners Local 454.

It was working with both executive and union laborers that provided her an insight into the effectiveness of networking. Cindy is as comfortable on the docks in a hard hat as she is at her desk in the president's office.

SIGN ME UP!

Belonging to and participating in trade and professional associations has always played an important role in Cindy's success. True, she enjoys the networking benefits, but she also contributes substantially in service to any organization of which she's a member. Her willingness to help organizations combined with her unusual talents has resulted in her being elected to key offices in many of the associations in which she is active.

She is currently President of the Society of American Military Engineers and President of the Board of Managers of the Seaman's Institute.

Additionally, Cindy is active in the Women's International Trade Association, The Association of Diving Contractors, The National Association of Women in Construction, The Greater Philadelphia Chamber of Commerce and the Small Business Advisory Council of the Federal Reserve Bank of Philadelphia. Cindy is also on the Port of Philadelphia Maritime Society Board of Governors.

PIONEERING

Feeling shut out from the networking possibilities available to male executives through private clubs, Cindy went to her network for a solution. She sought the support of those who were members of one of Philadelphia's most prestigious business clubs, the venerable Union League Club.

Her timing was right. She was included among the first several women to be accepted into the Union League. She was also a founding member of the Harbour League Club, a business and social club in Camden, New Jersey. The Club has many members in businesses along the shores of the Delaware river with interests in the various river front activities.

NETWORKING RESULTS

When asked for examples of how networking has been of specific help, Cindy related the story of her involvement in the Entrepreneurial Forum of Drexel University.

Here she met her counterpart who was working in a similar program at the University of Pennsylvania. It just happened this woman's husband was in charge of a large real estate project that had opportunities for Cindy's company. Networking had opened the door.

She told of another time when her company was involved in a claim with the Navy. The negotiations pitted Cindy against a Navy captain. The captain thought he had the advantage.

He soon, however, recognized the effectiveness of Cindy's networking as she had to opportunity to bring into the negotiations the names of military officers of equal or higher rank than his own.

It wasn't intentional name-dropping, but it quickly put Cindy on equal footing.

RECOGNITION

For her outstanding success in and contribution to her profession, Cindy Hudson received the Women's Business Enterprise Award from the United States Department of Transportation in Washington, DC. She also received the Small

Business Person of the Year Award from the Greater Philadelphia Chamber of Commerce.

SAY GOOD-BYE TO THE "GOOD OLD BOYS" NETWORK

For most of modern times men have had the advantage when it came to networking. Things have changed. Now, women increasingly are finding their way into all of the organizations that foster good networking, and more importantly, women are taking leadership positions in those very organizations.

It's about time we said "good-bye" to the "good old boys"!

Success
Story #7

Homemade Networking

When a house is more than a home

Raymond Wells
Architect
Raymond Wells Associates
Oradell, New Jersey

Ray Wells has been networking all of his working life. As a young and struggling architect he appreciated the need for a wide circle of acquaintances. It enabled him to expand the opportunities for contacts that would lead to assignments. Friends who might be building, builders who needed architects, bankers who knew of people who were going to build...the list goes on.

NETWORKING THROUGH ORGANIZATIONS

For Ray, one of the best ways to quickly develop new acquaintances was through regular contact at various organizational meetings.

He and his wife Betty are active in their church. Ray was a Sunday School teacher and departmental supervisor. He not only joined, but actively participated in many local civic, charitable and service organizations. "I feel that my business and I, personally, owe the community that supports us, a debt. Repayment can easily be in the form of support for that community," Ray says.

He's been a member of: The Oradell, NJ Planning Board; the Hackensack, NJ Hospital Building Committee; the Paramus, NJ Board of Education Bicycle & Safety Committee; The Board of Education Aesthetics Committee and Code of Ethics Committee. He was also General Solicitations Chairman for the Boy Scout Drive, Trustee for the Northern New Jersey March of Dimes and Trustee for the United Way of Bergen County, NJ.

Ray is currently involved with The George Washington Cemetery Association and the New Jersey Aviation Hall of Fame as a Trustee. He's on the Advisory Board of a local historical restoration project and the Board of a local community college.

Because of his talents and intense interest in the many organizations he belongs to, Ray has risen to the top offices in many of these groups. He's been President of the Paramus Chamber of Commerce, the Paramus Jaycees, and Vice President of the Paramus Boys Club.

PROFESSIONAL ASSOCIATIONS

In addition to civic and service organizations, Ray is extremely active in his professional associations. These include: the American Institute of Architects, The New Jersey Society of Architects and the Architects League of Northern New Jersey.

ROTARY

Perhaps Ray's first love and most intensive interest is Rotary. Rotary is a service organization of more than one million. Members conduct humanitarian projects, encourage high ethical standards in all vocations and work toward world understanding and peace.

In short order, after joining the Rotary Club of Paramus, New Jersey, Ray quickly moved up to club President. From there he went on to the post of District Governor and then to the Board of Directors of Rotary International. He served a two-year term with fellow Board members from twelve countries: The United States, Switzerland, Chile, Brazil, The Netherlands, England, New Zealand, Japan, Korea, Canada, India and Mexico. The Rotary Board administers to over a million Rotarians in 178 countries.

THE HOUSE THAT'S MORE THAN A HOME

In 1979 Ray came across a new, unique and truly potent networking tool – a house. Not just any ordinary house, but a house that would attract local, and even international attention. He has had visitors from more than a dozen countries. It is a house that would never be forgotten for those who visited it – and so too would its owners, Ray and Betty, not soon be forgotten.

The house which caught Ray's eye, and which he talked (conned) Betty into agreeing to let him buy, has 23 rooms and four and one half acres of ground! The house was the historic Blauvelt Mansion, a Victorian castle that was originally part of an eighty acre estate and a northern New Jersey landmark.

In addition to living in the house, (with six children and thirteen grandchildren coming and going, they need a BIG house) Ray works out of the house – his professional offices occupy one wing.

WORKING THE HOUSE

With a house this big, unique and well known, Ray and Betty have always felt it should be shared with the community. They very generously allow community charities to use the house for fundraising tours with as many as twelve hundred people coming through for one tour. The house has also been used for many charitable receptions and parties, sometimes with the addition of a tent in the yard where Ray and Betty have hosted more than 250 people for dinner.

It doesn't take much figuring to appreciate how many people find their way into the Wells' network because of their house.

LAUGHTER: THE BEST MEDICINE

Like most who have networked their way to success, Ray Wells uses more than one technique to build a network. As another facet of the artistic talent needed for his architecture, Ray is blessed with the ability to create cartoons. In place of standard greeting cards, Ray sends friends who are hospitalized humorous personalized cartoons exaggerating their situations and combining some of their special interests or hobbies. Usually he sends the cartoon in a three to five day series. Not only the recipients, but the doctors and nurses as well look forward to Ray's next get-well cartoon.

In spite of the time Ray spends doing things for other people, he still finds time to enjoy the fruits of his success: traveling, playing golf and tennis and enjoying his family.

Ray and Betty Wells are typical examples of people who have learned to "give themselves away."

A SAMPLE OF SOME OF RAY WELLS' UNIQUE GET WELL MESSAGES

Success Story #8

Networking and Partnering

Can they live together?

Rebecca Amble
Founder & President
Future Focus
A Marketing Consulting Organization
Saint Paul, Minnesota

Is it possible that we're writing about someone who has been quoted in the press as saying that she believes networking doesn't work and that she wonders if it ever did?

We *are* writing about Rebecca Amble, in spite of her statement and feelings about networking, because in fact Rebecca is an outstanding networker.

Her negative feelings about networking are based upon the concept of the "business card exchange networking" common to chambers of commerce and other organizations. It's the type of networking in which people meet, eat and exchange business cards strictly for the purpose of business and as their sole form of networking. Rebecca wonders if this is not selfish and ultimately unproductive. If this is the only type of networking one does, we share Rebecca's concern.

THE OTHER SIDE

Don Groen, president of the Bloomington, Minnesota Chamber of Commerce, had this to say at a networking forum, "The challenge is that most people don't know how to network. There's a skill to it. It's more than going up and saying, 'My name is Don Groen.' It's an ability to learn more about the person than just their name, what they do and what they sell.

"Many times we've seen business relationships develop as a result of networking," Groen continued. "It's as old as the hills, but sometimes we have to teach people how to network to keep those business relationships developing."

Actually Rebecca respects (and uses) networking within the context of our definition: *disciplined acquaintanceship.*

THE *PARTNER* PROCESS

If you expect to get a new account by handing out your cards at a luncheon or by playing golf at the country club, you're not behaving the way the marketplace expects, according to Rebecca. "Most people try to make a fast sale or find out to whom they should really be talking to make that sale," she says. "That approach ends up alienating the other person. You might as well put a 'gimme business' sign around your neck."

Rebecca Amble's approach to networking is to build relationships where both parties benefit. Her solution is a business development tool that she calls "partnering" and uses **P-A-R-T-N-E-R** as the acronym.

The ***P*** stands for *purpose,* which is mutual benefit.

The *A* is for *asking questions.* You need to learn about the other person, not only what he or she does, but what he or she needs that you can offer.

The *R* is for *respect* for the other person's comments and opinions.

The *T* is for *trust,* which is essential if you are sharing personal or confidential information.

The *N* is for *nurture,* which covers the "care and feeding" of the relationship.

The ***E*** is for *empathy*. Without empathy, you can't understand the other person's needs and concerns.

The final ***R*** is for *reciprocating*. Totally one-sided relationships don't go very far in business. The roles of giving and taking will change, and each person must play both roles.

"Before you set out for that golf game or the next association luncheon, define what your needs are and what your service is," Rebecca advises. "Then ask yourself, 'Who knows people who need my firm?' These are the people you want to partner with. The trick is identifying the people in the professions, companies or associations who can connect you to future business."

The next step is determining the benefit for your networking partner. Rebecca suggests that you be very direct about asking what the other person needs or wants from you.

"Keep in mind that you want a reason to maintain your relationship as long as it's agreeable to both parties," she says. "Direct business referrals are only one reason to have a networking partner."

Rebecca suggests these options as well:

- A relationship with a visionary who is on top of trends and issues in the marketplace and can act as your mentor.
- A connection with a key opinion leader who can challenge you and your ideas.
- A relationship with someone who shares your philosophy and provides you with support and encouragement.

PUBLIC RELATIONS NETWORKING

One of the most effective tools in Rebecca Amble's networking arsenal is her ability to "get ink" – to get her name and story into the press.

Consider that she was mentioned on the front page of both the ***Wall Street Journal*** and the "Life" section of ***USA Today***. She has appeared in articles in ***Working Mother, Working***

Woman, the ***Minneapolis-Saint Paul CityBusiness***, the ***Minneapolis Star Tribune***, the ***Saint Paul Pioneer Press*** and a host of other publications.

SPEAKING AND WORKSHOPS

Rebecca relies heavily upon another form of networking – speaking to business groups. You will find her speaking in a variety of settings, whether at the traditional after lunch or dinner situation, at seminars or at workshops. Her subjects include: Marketing Management, Market Research, Communications, Marketing Training, Developing a Partner Information Connection (P.I.C. System), and of course, her PARTNER concept.

She may call it the PARTNER process, but *we* think Rebecca Amble *networked* her way to success!

Success Story #9

Postcards from Kathmandu

International networking

Ray W. Jutkins
ROCKINGHAM*JUTKINS*marketing
Venice, California

Ray Jutkins is an unusual and exciting speaker, seminar leader writer and ad man. But more important for this book, Ray is a great networker.

Ken first met Ray in Australia where they shared the platform at the week-long Pan Pacific Direct Marketing Conference. Ken was impressed by Ray's presentation. Who wouldn't be impressed to see a speaker at a prestigious symposium address the audience in jeans and vest (it was actually a custom-made jeans suit) with a red checked shirt...and stocking feet! Combining a humorous introduction and explanation, his appearance worked. Ray grabbed the audience's attention. They learned and were entertained.

Ray no longer wears his jeans "uniform" when speaking, nor does he appear in stocking feet. However he'll wear both a tie patterned with a bit of red and a red-checked handkerchief in his breast pocket to tie in with his earlier presentations.

That's Ray's style – a combination of flair, learning and laughing to get the best results.

POSTCARDS FROM KATHMANDU

Considering Ray's imaginative presentations and writing, you could almost predict his creative networking. Shortly after an exchange of business cards in Australia, Ken received the first of Ray's many networking efforts – it was a postcard from Kathmandu.

Ray had traveled there in connection with a meeting he was participating in for American Express Travel Service in Manila. His postcard showed a full-color picture of Mount Everest in the Himalayas. On the other side, the address half of the post card was labeled with the address (prepared in advance of the trip), and with postage represented by two beautiful stamps from Malaysia, where the cards had been mailed.

The message side of the card had some information about his trip printed in the upper left hand corner, much as you would see on a typical travel post card. Next to this message was a small picture of Ray. His handwritten and personal message followed. Printed at the bottom of the card were the logo, mailing address and phone information for his company and a list of services offered.

The post card served several purposes. It was certainly an advertising vehicle, but to many who received the card, it was also a personal message from a friend or acquaintance from an exciting place. Surely many of those who received his card saved the stamps.

That card was the beginning of a long series of cards from Ray from around the world. Most came with personal messages and some with pre-printed stock messages which were applicable to his entire name list.

Ray has used the cover of his book, ***Direct Marketing: How You Can Really Do It Right*** on postcards sent for year-end greetings and for seminar announcements.

True, there's some expense involved in sending the post cards, and certainly a great deal of planning and preparation, but the results are electric. You won't soon forget "Rocket" Ray.

BUCK SLIP NOTES

In addition to the pre-planned postcard, another of Ray's networking tools is the *buck slip note*. This is a brief note written or typed on a small (5.5" X 8.5") piece of stationery or tablet paper, printed with Ray's name at the top and corporate address information at the bottom. Like his postcards, the buck slips are written on a regular "keep-in-touch" basis. Buck slips are easy to write, and they give a special feeling of being more personal than a letter. They're ideal for short notes. And Ray capitalizes on the speed and attention-getting advantages of the fax to send electronic buck slips.

Ray says, "I like to reach out (just like E.T.) and 'touch.' The fax and mailbox really work for me."

"TASTEFUL" NETWORKING

Baskin-Robbins, maker of great ice cream, is a promotion oriented company. Ray tied in with them and uses their free coupons as a networking device. The coupons are for a free, double scoop, Baskin-Robbins ice cream cone, and they are imprinted with, "Compliments of ROCKINGHAM* JUTKINS* marketing" and the phone number. The coupons can be redeemed at any Baskin-Robbins store. Ray gives them out with his business card when meeting new people.

"Can you forget someone who gives you an ice cream cone?" asks Ray. "It leaves most people with a good taste in their mouth!"

BIG LEAGUE NETWORKING

In his quest for creative ways to promote himself and his agency, Ray came across personalized sports cards – a take-off of the popular collectors' baseball cards.

Ray is pictured on one side of the card, posed with a glove and ball. The other side of the card lists Ray's "stats":

Bats: Right • Throws: Right
Born: Orange, NJ

Direct Marketing's answer to hustling Pete Rose and "Ironman" Lou Gehrig, "Rocket" Ray Jutkins has parlayed his prodigious knowledge and boundless enthusiasm into legendary successes for many of North America's best known direct marketers.

Since 1965, no one has matched Ray's unique record of success in combining direct marketing savvy, direct mail and telemarketing know-how to produce successful programs for clients in the financial, industrial, computer, travel, insurance and telecommunications industries.

MAJOR LEAGUE PROFILE

Ray has been a member of the US Olympic Swimming Committee and a manager of the Pan-American and World Championship swimming teams. An energetic traveler, Ray has circled the globe visiting over 90 countries on all seven continents.

"Rocket" Ray Jutkins, through his creative promotions, has proven himself to be a major league networker!

Success Story #10

A Dual Career

Seminar networking

Kathleen Flynn Peterson, RN
Robbins, Kaplan, Miller & Ciresi
Minneapolis, Minnesota

Synergy can be defined as two actions working together to produce a result more powerful than the sum of its parts. In the case of Kathleen Flynn Peterson, the combination of her two professional backgrounds has produced a new professional posture with greater potential than either of her individual careers.

NURSE AND LAWYER

Kathleen began her practice of law with a background as a registered nurse. Her goal was to develop a law practice emphasizing her experience with nursing, concentrating on the areas of medical malpractice and medical products litigation. She was fortunate to join a very reputable law firm with a different practice areas in a several nation-wide locations.

The partners in the medical litigation department had excellent reputations, and Kathleen's assumption was that cases referred to the firm would be referred to them directly. In order for her to develop her own clientele, she knew it would be necessary to develop an independent reputation as a competent and successful litigator within the firm.

EXPERT WITNESSES

A successful medical malpractice and medical products liability practice requires the availability of expert witnesses. These are people who can assist litigators in evaluation of cases. They also serve as witnesses at the respective trials of the various cases. Thus, the goal of developing this practice area requires developing a strong network of medical expert witnesses.

Kathleen's marketing strategy was to differentiate herself from other litigators and to stress her nursing background. She chose to begin marketing her practice to a group she was very comfortable with and a group with whom she would have a great deal of credibility – nurses.

Nurses in the state of Minnesota have continuing education requirements in order to keep their licenses. Kathleen contacted each hospital inservice director in the state of Minnesota as well as the organizations which were offering continuing education courses for nursing. She advised them of her background, experience and willingness to make presentations to nurses regarding the legal aspects of nursing practice. The offer for her presentations was made with no strings attached, they would be free of charge.

THE SEMINAR CONCEPT

At each seminar Kathleen provided the participants with her name and phone number and offered to answer any questions the participants had following the seminar, or in the future – again without any charge to them.

Through the presentations to nurses, she was able to develop a network of individuals who knew of her skills as an attorney, and at the same time develop her vast network of expert witnesses. At every lecture, she would receive contacts for future lectures. Soon she was giving frequent lectures to large audiences of nurses. Nurses were telling their friends, families, colleagues and patients about Kathleen's services as an attorney with a strong medical background. Soon she was receiving many more case referrals. As her practice enlarged, she began receiving many more invitations to speak than she could really accept. To solve that problem, she produced a videotape of her seminar. The videotape was marketed independently and was also offered to individuals who had invited her to lecture when she was not personally able to speak.

SIDE EFFECTS

Just as synergy played an significant role in the combining of her two careers, so too did it play an important role in the combination of seminars and video presentations.

The contacts she made during those presentations served to substantially enlarge her network of referrals as well as expert witnesses. She also gained a great deal of experience in public speaking, a bonus which helped enhance her skills as a trial advocate.

Success Story #11

Take the Elevator to Success

Four stops on the way up

Edwin E. Bobrow CMC,
President
Bobrow Consulting Group, Inc.
New York, NY

Ed Bobrow's company specializes in marketing and marketing management to such clients as Honeywell, Dow Corning, Gilette and Norelco.

Additionally, Ed is an Adjunct Assistant Professor at New York University. He lectures extensively to businesses, trade associations and universities. He has written 5 books and over 100 articles on sales and marketing.

Ed is founder and president of Bobrow-Lewell Associates, a highly successful manufacturers' representative organization in New York. He credits networking with helping him achieve specific goals in all of his various endeavors.

We discussed with Ed the networking techniques he found most helpful as he built his various businesses to their current successes.

FOUR NETWORKING TECHNIQUES

There are four specific things which come to mind when we think of Ed Bobrow's networking technique. He was one of the pioneers in using die-cut letterheads and business cards. (Die cutting is part of the printing process where a sharp steel die cuts the paper in a desired design.) Ed used a bold letter "B" at the top right hand side of his stationary and business card. The die-cut came around part of the "B" and the rest extended beyond the edge of the paper. It was attention-getting and provided long memory retention value to his correspondence and for his business card.

Ed also took advantage of color and used a distinctive shade of brown for all of his printed materials. People who received either his letters or business cards almost always mentioned how original they were. It was simply a matter of using components of the networking process – letter writing and business cards – and adding a unique touch.

THE ELEVATOR TRICK

Next Ed developed his *elevator* introductions. It is important to know how to properly introduce yourself in an elevator and how to hold a conversation before you reach your floor. Everybody's had it happen at trade shows or conventions. You get on the elevator and someone sees your badge. "Oh, you're from the XYZ company," they say, "and what do you do?"

Ed has had to prepare himself to be able to give a quick but effective answer along with his card before the car reaches one of the stops. He states that your ability to quickly describe who you are and what you do is an important networking technique for almost any kind of chance meeting.

THANK YOU CARDS

Another networking technique is one Ed calls "drop a card for a card."

Here's how it works. Every time you receive a business card that you expect will have some value or that you expect to keep and file, you respond by sending that person a post card or note reminding them of the occasion of the card exchange and something that might have happened in connection it. "Thank you for sharing some time with me at lunch yesterday," or "Thank you for the valuable ideas you shared with me at the meeting this morning," or "I really appreciated the good service you gave me."

Remember, people like to be thanked. It's an important key to building respect and friendships.

NEWSLETTERS

The fourth networking concept that comes to mind may be the most effective one for identifiable results. That's Ed's use of newsletters.

Ed has been using them for years. They continually bring him both good contacts and actual assignments. First of all, he doesn't charge for them. And he doesn't publish them on a regular basis. That eliminates the problem of people expecting them when he might not be ready to publish for many reasons.

Ed always tries to incorporate helpful information along with news of what his company doing. And he does a little advertising for both his clients and himself. Often he'll write about situations where he's trying to put people and companies, or companies and companies together. To protect confidentiality, he describes the situations but codes them for replies. This system has really worked well for Ed, with responses often coming long after the receipt of the newsletters. Newsletters have a greater memory retention value than most people appreciate.

It's been fascinating to watch how Ed Bobrow has networked his way to success.

Success Story #12

High Tech Networking

Networking for profit and charity

Don Crescimanno
Executive Director
Cat-Net, Calendar Announced TeleNetwork
Honolulu, Hawaii

A physicist in Hawaii networking with over 5,000 people a week? Hardly.

But it's true!

Don Crescimanno started as a salesperson in the computer business in 1966 when, in Don's words, "computers were doing only very boring stuff – payrolls, taxes, massive inventories and scientific projects."

Computers may have been doing boring things, but Don still had to find ways to sell them.

In an effort to create some variety, Don came up with several *exciting* uses for computers, including marketing, and social networking. In 1975 he designed a data base/word processing software for a desk top computer. It enabled a sales person to make thousands of contacts a week versus the ten to twenty formerly made in the same amount of time. The goal of the system was a face-to-face contact with a qualified prospect.

Many people are involved in the buying decision for expensive and complicated computers. As a salesperson, Don recognized that you have to network with a client's business and get everybody interested – from management through purchasing, design, applications and engineering personnel.

Once sold, these same people become part of his network and were prospects for additional equipment and programs.

IT'S PARTY TIME!

Don developed a unique concept which generated the necessary networking process – a networking party of prospects. Engineers, mathematicians, physicists & programers were all invited to the supplier's special conference room for an elegant buffet – the perfect setting for lively discussion of applications and problem solving – and for networking.

Don is not one to let grass grow under his feet. Feeling the need for a challenge, he moved to Hawaii and carried his computerized "invitation to a party" concept with him. Only this time he adapted it to the social scene for both fun & profit.

In his new environment, Don had to start from scratch. His problem was one he'd faced before – he needed to know his prospective customers' problems and goals prior to the introduction of product.

How does one get to know customers face-to-face prior to he initiation of the sales cycle?

ELECTRONIC NETWORKING

Don had already realized that people enjoy meeting others with like minded interests. Keeping this in mind, he put together social functions – inviting successful business and professional people. He became a people broker. The critical ingredient in Don's events was not the place, the food or the entertainment...it was the interesting, motivated people invited. These events became a real hit (and a great source of prospects for Don).

As these events became more and more popular, Don realized that he needed some assistance. He notes, "My computer data base allowed me to keep track of our highly mobile Honolulu business and professional population. However, manually calling fifty to a hundred or a thousand people a week started to drain my resources of time and energy.

"I looked into the possibility of voice mail and voice mail boxes. The existing commercial equipment was just too expensive. Turning to my technical training I put together my own equipment and software to serve my own special and very personal needs.

"With what I believed to be a good product and efficient equipment I launched Cat-Net (Calendar Announced Tele-Network)."

CALENDAR ANNOUNCED TELE-NETWORK

Cat-Net is a for-profit social networking system. It provides members with a voice calendar of events in many areas of interest, and it can be accessed from any touch tone phone 24 hours a day.

The content of the Cat-Net Calendar is based on Don's careful review of newspapers, magazines, TV, newsletters, and the public and private sources of Cat-Net members.

Every member can update his or her personal calendar of business, professional and social events for an entire week with a three minute phone call.

Additionally, Don invites members to events by three means: first by calling the Cat-Net Calendar (voice mail), by being invited by Don's sophisticated automatic dialing computer or by mailed invitations. Members must have their own personal answering machine. The sponsoring individuals for events need an answering machine for accumulating the R.S.V.P.'s.

Membership in Cat-Net is by referral. Membership information is not offered through general advertising. The desire is to attract select individuals anxious to participate. Those seeking membership can contact an existing member for sponsorship.

Don asks individual members to exercise care and judgement when inviting guests to functions. He says, "We are creating an organizational personality which is the sum of its individual parts." Membership is revocable if a member abuses the computer access system. There is an annual membership fee to access the Calendar and to receive weekly event announcements and invitations.

SOCIAL EVENTS

Don says there are an average of 550 events going on in Honolulu each week. Additionally he may stage as many as 200 member events a year including private parties, theatre parties, cruises, art openings, club and restaurant openings and charity events.

Perhaps the most popular Cat-Net events are the Tuesday night business mixers. These events consist of between 150 and 400 business people and professionals attending a mixer cocktail party at a different restaurant location every week. Here people network and gather both leads and social contacts. Members pay a modest admission charge and pay for their drinks. The restaurant provides the hors d'oeurves. (Co-author Ken Erdman has attended one of these Tuesday night mixers and reports that they are everything promised – a great way to business network each week in some of the finest Honolulu restaurants and clubs.)

SOCIAL ENTERTAINMENT

Thursday evenings are the time for social entertainment functions, plays, concerts, art openings, movie premiers and stage events. Thursday evenings are also very popular with professionals and business people.

Other events include beach and boat parties, dinner parties, wine tastings, holiday parties, anniversaries and theme parties (which are always a special challenge to Don).

We asked Don to describe a couple of typical events to which one might be invited. Don described a wine tasting party hosted by a friend and member. It's a sumptuous wine tasting held every year with more than 750 people invited to Don's friend's home for hors d'oeurves and wines from around the world. "He has money," Don says, "and the place to hold such an event, but he is unable to spend the time required to select and invite the guests. So he leaves it to my discretion. These gatherings have now become the basis for his social and business calendar for the ensuing year."

Sailor John is a retired sea captain who enjoys taking as many as fifty guests out for a picnic sail on his 89 foot catch. He enjoys sailing, but he really enjoys entertaining. Owning an auto parts distributing company doesn't allow John the time to round up 25 to 50 guests for his weekend sails, so he relies on Don and his network to provide the guests.

NETWORKING FOR CHARITY

Often Cat-Net is called on to help with charitable causes, and Don Crescimanno is quick to respond. He notes, "As a volunteer fund raiser for several community organizations, I have access to the Who's Who in Honolulu corporate, small business, professional, political and service organizations."

The Variety Club of Honolulu wanted to donate a brand new van for the use of a worthwhile children's organization for a full year. The chairperson, being new to the Island, didn't know where to turn for qualified applicants. Don, with his vast network was able the very day he was contacted to put the chairperson in personal touch with a reputable organization who could really benefit from the use of the van

It was a typical example of the charitable side of Cat-Net.

NETWORKING REWARDS

Don sums up his networking experiences this way, "The real fun in my business is the very interesting successful people I am able to meet and introduce to one another. A French chef never had as much pleasure as I do in creating 'possibilities through people,' a stew which only gets better with age as new individual ingredients are added."

Success
Story #13

The Ronald McDonald House

Networking and prayer

Jim Murray, President
Jim Murray Limited
Sports Marketing – Public Relations Consultants

In the beginning, a young child, Kim Hill, was diagnosed with leukemia. Her father, Fred, a former All-American at Southern Cal and a professional football player with the Philadelphia Eagles, was devastated but found great consolation with immediate help from his neighbors and teammates.

To help defray Kim's medical expenses at St. Christopher's Hospital in Philadelphia, an insurance executive, Stan Lane, and neighbors of Fred's started a non-profit organization which was named Eagles Fly for Leukemia. At the initial fund raiser, a dinner dance in New Jersey, Fred's neighbors, local business people and his teammates all joined to raise money for St. Christopher's.

ENTER JIM MURRAY

Leonard Tose, the owner of the Philadelphia Eagles, and Pete Retzlaff, the general manager of the Eagles, wanted to involve the Eagles in Fly for Leukemia in a much deeper way. They assigned assistant PR director Jim Murray to head the project. Jim would start a network including friends, players, doctors, and just about anybody else that could help. Murray, a deeply religious man, turned to prayer for help with this very special project.

A planning meeting included Kim's doctor of hematology, Dr. Lory Naiman. One of the answers to Jim's prayers came with Dr. Naiman's selfless act of saying they have great needs at St. Christopher's hospital but there is someone with a greater need. He directed Jim to call the Chief of Oncology at Children's Hospital in Philadelphia, Dr. Audrey Evans.

THE HIGH FLYING EAGLES

Leonard Tose pledged $1 million for the Eagles to raise to help furnish the new leukemia floor at Children's Hospital. After the initial promotion, a second dinner dance was held which included further participation from the Eagles team. Team members involved included head coach, Ed Khayat, quarterback Roman Gabriel, and wide receiver, Harold Carmichael. The initial goal of $50,000 was surpassed, and the first check for $125,000 was donated through Eagles Fly for Leukemia to Children's Hospital.

THE RONALD MCDONALD HOUSE

The check was presented at the famous Blue Line Restaurant in the Spectrum arena, home of the Philadelphia Flyers and '76ers. As Dr. Evans accepted the check, she uttered those words that would give birth to the miracle of the Ronald McDonald House. She said, "Wouldn't it be great if there was a place for families to share their feelings when one of their children gets really sick and has to be hospitalized. In other words a place where families whose lives have been shattered by a cancer diagnosis or other serious disease, could find a place to stay that could replicate their home."

Guided, he felt, by prayer, Jim Murray called his friend Don Tuckerman, an account executive at the Elkman Advertising

Agency of Philadelphia. Jim asked him what he thought of Dr. Evans' suggestion and if it could fit into one of Elkman's accounts – perhaps McDonald's. Murray's next question for Tuckerman was: What's your next promotion for McDonald's? It turned out to be St. Patrick's Day Shamrock Shakes. Could the sale of Shamrock Shakes be somehow tied in to raising money for the house?

Tuckerman said that he would contact the local co-op (local owners of McDonald's franchises and the regional office). He called back after talking to people like Frank Quinn and Chris Gabriel, local owner-operators, and regional manager, Ed Rensi. They loved the idea of helping raise money for a house for families of very ill children. They not only said yes to participating, but suggested calling the house the Ronald McDonald House. These businessmen promised to donate all of the proceeds from the Shamrock Shakes to help get the house going. It was a case of the green shakes producing some green money for a wonderful cause.

RONALD MCDONALD HOUSE EXPANDS

Babe, the daughter of local Philadelphia builder John Canuso, had been stricken with leukemia. She was being treated by Dr. Evans. A miracle happened when Dr. Evans put Jim Murray and John Canuso together. Together they found a house which John's family completely rehabilitated in three weeks.

The first Ronald McDonald House opened on October 15, 1974. The opening was special because the founder of McDonald's, Ray Kroc, attended. He would eventually play a major part in the house expanding all over the world.

One and a half years later, Jim Murray got a call from Pat Healy of Golin Communications (McDonald's P.R. firm). She advised him that there was a chance to make a major presentation to the McDonald's local dealers co-op in Chicago. This was a big step toward a second house.

Jim, through his football network, got the Chicago Bears owner Mike McCaskey to send him two guardian angels – a lawyer from Chicago, Charles Marino, and his wife Gaye. The

Marinos' daughter had been diagnosed with leukemia and was being treated by Dr. Edward Baum. Dr. Baum told the family of the Ronald McDonald House, and talked them into coming with him to Philadelphia to see it. What they saw was a real miracle – and something that could perhaps be duplicated in Chicago.

In order to prepare for the big meeting for a Ronald McDonald House in Chicago, Murray put together a team including Dr. Audrey Evans, Dr. Edward Baum, Eagles player Bill Bergy (Bill replaced Roman Gabriel as spokesperson for the campaign), Russ Wheeler (local McDonald's operator), Don Tuckerman and Bill McGrane (PR Director for the Chicago Bears) and two other couples whose children were being treated at Children's Memorial Hospital in Chicago. The Chicago co-op said yes, conducted a promotion with Orange Crush soft drink and transformed a convent at St. Clement's Parish of Chicago into a new $1 million Ronald McDonald House, the second of its kind.

Within the past 19 years, 150 Ronald McDonald Houses have been opened throughout the world. These homes provide temporary housing for about 450,000 people a year in the United States, Canada, Australia and Europe. With networking, starting at the very top, with the Lord answering Jim Murray's prayers and the continued support of Ed Rensi, now President of McDonald's, the miracle continues.

Success
Story #14

Networking the Liberty Bell

The rewards of service

Edward Piszek
Founder, Mrs. Paul's Kitchens

Back in 1988, Ken Erdman was Chairman of the annual Rotary International Convention. That year the convention was to be held in Philadelphia, and Ken was in search of a replica of the Liberty Bell. His concept was to decorate the lower level of the Philadelphia Civic Center as Independence Mall – the most historic square mile in the country. This was the space to be used for the convention's "House of Friendship" where people from more than 100 countries would meet and visit.

The two major points of interest in Independence Mall are Independence Hall and the Liberty Bell. Ken could contract to have a one-dimensional facade of Independence Hall built, but he wanted a three-dimensional Liberty Bell – and hopefully one that would actually ring.

NETWORKING TO THE RESCUE

With a networking phone call to Tom Muldoon, president of the Philadelphia Visitors and Convention Bureau, Ken learned that Edward Piszek, the founder of Mrs. Paul's Kitchens, headed a charitable and patriotic group called The Liberty Bell Foundation. The Foundation has a metal replica of the Liberty Bell, weighing several tons and cast in the foundry in England that cast the original Liberty Bell. And yes, it could be rung. But, suggested Tom, it might not be an easy job to get the bell for a week-long convention.

Networking to the rescue. Ken wrote Ed Piszek a note and told him of his need. The day the note was received, Ed called Ken and asked him to stop by and give him some more information. When Ken told Ed the dates the bell would be needed, Ken learned that the bell was to be used as part of a Southern state's historical celebration. But Ed was so impressed and excited with the thought of sharing the bell with international visitors, he called and rearranged the schedule for the bell so it could be used at the Rotary International convention.

Through the generosity of Ed Piszek and the Liberty Bell Foundation, the bell made its appearance at the convention. Ed and the Foundation provided the bell complete with move-in and move-out transportation, insurance coverage and several people to assist visitors and ring the bell during the convention.

NOT THE END OF THE STORY

Now this could be the end of the story – but, with networking, the process is always on-going. As a result of working on the convention project together, Ken and Ed became friends. Ken had read much in the Philadelphia papers about Ed's many philanthropic endeavors. Their new friendship gave Ken the opportunity to learn much more about the impact of networking on Ed's world-wide business, charitable and service contributions.

BUSINESS NETWORKING

Ed started on his journey to business success from a tiny kitchen behind a bar in the industrial section of Philadelphia. He prepared what was probably the first frozen seafood anywhere. His first frozen crabs were done in the ice compartment of a small refrigerator. From there he went on to become known world-wide for his frozen packaged seafood.

Networking mentors were an important part of Ed's business life. He likened them to father figures, who made up for the father he had lost. He often called on these mentors for advice, understanding and encouragement.

CHURCH NETWORKING

While Ed owned Mrs. Paul's Kitchens, the company was producing documentaries with James A. Michener for Public Broadcasting TV Stations.

A documentary, "Poland – The Will to Be," was in production, and a special part of the film was to be dedicated to the Catholic Church in Poland. The film described how religion had prevailed in Poland despite the presence of Communism since 1945.

The production company wanted to interview Primate Cardinal Wyszynski in Warsaw for the film. Since the Cardinal spoke only Polish, Ed thought it might be interesting to interview Cardinal Wojtyla of Krakow, who spoke fluent English. A networking phone call was made to Cardinal Wojtyla (whom Ed Piszek and James Michener had never met or really knew of). From that phone call, a meeting was arranged and Cardinal Wojtyla agreed to be interviewed.

That interview became a very important and historical part of the film. A few years later, while attending a meeting in Poland with many participants, Ed received a phone call from Rome informing him that Cardinal Wojtyla had just been elected Pope. Since then Ed has visited with the Holy Father on numerous occasions.

GOVERNMENT NETWORKING

During a conversation about the future of Poland, Polish Deputy Minister of Education Andrezj Janowski told Ed, "If I could have 400 English teacher in Poland, I could have 10 million Poles speaking English by the year 2000." This was at the time when President Bush had announced he was sending 60 teachers to Hungary and 60 to Poland.

Ed's initial calculations told him that the cost of sending 400 teachers to Poland was enormous and unattainable. Then he thought of the Peace Corps.

Ed had a friend in Washington named Tom Sneeringer who was the top aide to Congressman Dan Rostenkowski. Again, with a networking phone call from Ed to Tom, and another call from Dan Rostenkowski to Paul Coverdell, director of the Peace Corps, Ed was on his way to Washington for a meeting with Mr. Coverdell. From this meeting, a Peace Corps Partners in Teaching English program was developed. Currently there are 192 teachers in Poland.

Ed Piszek says: "Much of the success of our program can be credited to phone calls and letters to friends, acquaintances and mentors from my business, social, church and government networks.

THE ROTARY AWARD FOR WORLD UNDERSTANDING

In 1991, Ken Erdman, as a Past Director of Rotary International, was on the nomination committee to select a person for Rotary's highest honor, The Rotary Award for International Understanding.

This award is granted annually by Rotary International to an individual whose life or work exemplifies the Rotary Ideal of Service in the promotion of international understanding, goodwill and peace.

Rotary has been a leader in the field of humanitarian service and in the promotion of international goodwill. Therefore the organization deemed it appropriate to grant recognition to individuals who exemplify this service ideal, not only as a tribute to their work and contributions, but also to present a worthy example for others to follow.

As a member of the nominating committee for the award, Ken had the opportunity to recommend one candidate. As he considered potential candidates, thinking mostly of world-known figures, Ken remembered his friend Edward Piszek. Did his nomination have to be a world-known figure? Who, he thought, could be more deserving? And so he did some research into Ed's possible qualifications. What Ken found impressed him even further. He decided to put forth the name of Edward Piszek for consideration by the selection committee (which was made up of the joint committee of the Board of Directors of both Rotary International and the Trustees of The Rotary Foundation).

In November of 1991, three years after Ken and Ed met, the President of Rotary International wrote Ed Piszek (in part):

Dear Mr. Piszek:

It is my honor, as President of Rotary International, to notify you that you are the 1991-92 recipient of the Rotary Award for World Understanding.

The award is Rotary's highest honor. It is given each year to an individual whose life, or work, exemplifies the Rotary Ideal of Service, especially in the promotion of international understanding, goodwill and peace. The Rotary Board of Directors and the Trustees of the Rotary Foundation selected you for this award because of your ceaseless work to help the people of Poland, your work through Americares, and your numerous other philanthropic activities. Your life demonstrates the miraculous results of work carried out with vision, commitment and love.

In accepting this award, you will join a list of past recipients that includes Pope John Paul II, Vaclev Havel, the President of Czechoslovakia, and Javier Perez de Cuellar, the Secretary General of the United Nations.

We would like you to consider lending your name to some of our Rotary Foundation activities. If agreeable, $250,000 of Foundation projects and/or scholarships in your areas of interest would bear your name.

Sincerely,
Rajendra K. Saboo,
President

It seems appropriate to end our book with this story, a story that truly presents the unique possibilities of networking. We hope it proves that you really can ***Network Your Way To Success!***

Toolbox

A SELECTION OF BOOKS FOR THE SERIOUS NETWORKER

All Chapters

Network Your Net Worth, by Tom Sullivan
published by Networthing, Inc.

The Network Strategy, by Malcolm Nichol
published by Univite, Inc.

Chapters One through Five

Is Your "Net" Working?, by Anne Boe
published by John Wiley & Sons, Inc.

You and Your Network, by Fred Smith
published by Ivy Books

Smart People: A User's Guide to Experts, by John D. Spooner
published by Little, Brown & Company

Chapter One

Power Shift, by Alvin Toffler
published by Bantam Books

Megatrends, by John Naisbitt
published by Warner Books

Megatrends 2000, by John Naisbitt and Patricia Aburdene
published by William Morrow & Co., Inc.

The Networking Book, by Jessica Lipnack and Jeffrey Stamps
published by Viking Penguin

Re-Inventing the Corporation, by John Naisbitt
published by Warner Books

Chapter Two

Corporate Networking, by Robert K. Mueller
published by The Free Press

The Aquarian Conspiracy, by Marilyn Ferguson
published by J. P. Tarcher

Chapter Three

How to Work a Room, by Susan Roane
published by Warner Books

All I Really Need to Know I Learned in Kindergarten
by Robert Fulghum
published by Ballantine Books

It Was On Fire When I Lay Down On It, by Robert Fulghum
published by Villard Books

Games People Play, by Eric Berne, M.D.
published by Ballantine Books

Chapter Five

The Great Brain Robbery, by Ray Considine and Murray Raphel
published by The Great Brain Robbery

Chapter Eight

Mind Your Own Business!, by Murray Raphel
published by Raphel Marketing

The Harvey Mackay Rolodex® Network Builder, by Harvey B. Mackay
published by Rolodex® Corporation

Swim With the Sharks Without Being Eaten Alive, by Harvey Mackay
published by Ivy Books

The Address Book, by Michael Levine
published by Perigee Press

Chapter Nine

Power Talking, by George R. Walther
published by G. P. Putnam's Sons

Phone Power, by George R. Walther
published by G. P. Putnam's Sons

You Can Sell Anything By Telephone!, by Dr. Gary S. Goodman
published by Prentice-Hall

Telephone Marketing, by Murray Roman
published by McGraw-Hill Book Company

Successful Telephone Selling in the '80's
by Martin D. Shafiroff and Robert L. Shook
published by Harper & Row Publishers

Selling Your Services, by Robert W. Bly
published by Henry Holt & Company

Chapter Ten

How to Close Every Sale, by Joe Girard
published by Warner Books

Chapter Eleven

Direct Marketing: How You Can Really Do It Right!
by "Rocket" Ray Jutkins
published by HDL Publishing

The Do-It-Yourself Direct Mail Handbook
by Murray Raphel & Ken Erdman
published by Marketers Bookshelf

Small Business Guide to Direct Mail, by Lin Grensing
published by Self-Counsel Press

Direct Mail Magic, by Charles Mallory
published by Crisp Publications

Chase's Annual Events
published by Contemporary Books

America Celebrates
published by Visible Ink Press

Chapter Twelve

High Visibility, by Irving Rein, Philip Kolter & Martin Stoller
published by Dodd Mead & Company

The Zen of Hype: An Insider's Guide to the Publicity Game
by Raleigh Pinskey
published by Carol Publishing Group

Street Smart Marketing, by Jeff Slutsky
published by John Wiley & Sons, Inc.

Do•It•Yourself Publicity, by David F. Ramacitti
published by American Management Association

Getting Publicity: A Do-It-Yourself Guide for Small Business and Non-Profit Groups, by Tana Fletcher and Julia Rockler
published by Self-Counsel Press

Chapter Thirteen

Marketing With Newsletters, by Elaine Floyd
published by EF Communications

How to Make $25,000 a Year Publishing Newsletters
by Brian T. Sheehan
published by Parker Publishing Co., Inc.

Fundamentals of Successful Newsletters, by Thomas H. Bivens
published by NTC Business Books

Chapter Fourteen

Specialty Advertising, New Dimensions in Creative Marketing
by George Herfel & Steve Slack
published by Specialty Advertising Association International

Chapter Fifteen

Beyond the Bottom Line, by Claude Farley, Ph.D.
published by McGraw-Hill Publishing Company

Chapter Sixteen

Trade Show Basics, by Norman Abelson
published by Commerce Communications, Inc.

The Successful Exhibitors Handbook, by Barry Siskind
published by Self-Counsel

Chapter Seventeen

Read With Me, by Walter Anderson
published by Houghton Mifflin Company

Chapter Nineteen

Congratulations! You've Been Fired!
by Emily Koltnow and Lynne S. Dumas
published by Fawcett Columbine

The Resume Catalog, by Yana Parker
published by Ten Speed Press

What Color is Your Parachute?, by Richard Boller
published by Ten Speed Press

How to Market Yourself, by David E. Drive
published by The Noble Press, Inc.

Knock 'Em Dead – With Great Answers to Tough Interview Questions
by Martin Yate
published by Bob Adams, Inc.

Chapter Twenty-One

How to Win Friends and Influence People, by Dale Carnegie
published by Pocket Books

What Do You Say After You Say Hello?, by Eric Berne, M.D.
published by Bantam Books

Chapter Twenty-Five

The Good Heart Book – A Guide to Volunteering, by David E. Drive
published by The Noble Press, Inc.

Try Giving Yourself Away, by David Dunn
published by Prentice Hall

Chapter Twenty-Six

Tough Selling for Tough Times, by Murray Raphel & Neil Raphel
published by Raphel Marketing

Seven Pillars of Sales Success, by Jonathan Evetts
published by Sterling Publishing Company, Inc.

Direct Sales: Be Better Than Good, Be GREAT! , by Joyce M. Ross
published by Pelican

Ziglar on Selling, by Zig Ziglar
published by Oliver-Nelson Books

Competitive Selling: A Fundamental Approach, by Josh Gordon
published by Cowles Business Media, Inc.

Beyond the Bottom Line, by Claude Farley, Ph.D.
published by McGraw-Hill Publishing Company

Compelling Selling, by Josh Gordon
published by Business Media, Inc.

Cold Calling Techniques (That Really Work!), by Stephan Schiffman
published by Bob Adams, Inc.

Network Sales Business, by Gregory Kishel & Patricia Kishel
published by John Wiley & Sons, Inc.

Success Story #8

Growth Partnering, by Mack Hanan
published by Amacom

MAGAZINE READING LIST FOR NETWORKERS

Business Week
published by: McGraw-Hill, Inc., NY, NY
800-635-1200

Fortune
published by: Time, Inc. Magazine Company, NY, NY
800-621-8000

Forbes
published by: Forbes, Inc., NY, NY
800-888-9896

Entrepreneur
published by: Entrepreneur, Inc.
714-261-2325

Personal Selling Power
published by: Personal Selling Power, Inc.
800-752-7355

Success
published by: Hal Holdings Corporation, NY, NY
800-234-7324

Sales and Marketing Management
published by: Bill Communications, Inc., New York, NY
212-986-4800

INC Magazine
published by: Goldhirsh Group, Inc.
800-234-0999

AUDIO TAPE SOURCES FOR NETWORKERS

Contact the following organizations for information and catalogs:

Audio Editions – Books on cassette; 800-231-4261

Discovery Seminars – "Power Networking"; 713-589-1989

Hoke Communications – Direct marketing & business; 800-645-6132

American Management Assn. – Business management skills
518-891-5510

Newstrack Executive Tape Service – Current business information & articles; 800-525-8289

King Street Recording Company – "Caring Customer Service"
215-647-4341

HCI Audio Library – Marketing; 800-229-6700

Books on Tape – Literature library, free 247 page catalog; 800-626-3333

Burg Communications, Inc. – Networking skills; 800-726-3667

Audio Forum – Personal development; 800-243-1234

Organizational Technologies – Successful selling; 800-423-1169

Simon & Schuster Audio Cassette Catalog – Business skills, fiction, personal development; 515-284-6755

Zig Ziglar Corporation – Business and Personal Motivation
3330 Earhart • Carrollton, TX 75006

Top Business Books on Tape (as listed in *Fortune* magazine)

The 7 Habits of Highly Effective People, by Stephen R. Covey
Swim With the Sharks, by Harvey Mackay
The 110% Solution, by Mark McCormack
Thriving on Chaos, by Tom Peters
The Japan That Can Say No, by Shintaro Ishihara
The Power Point, by Michael E. Gerber

VIDEO TAPE SOURCES FOR NETWORKERS

Bottom Line, Inc. – Tools for business and personal development
212-989-TAPE (8273)

CareerTrack Seminars & Tapes – Career enhancement and personal development; 800-334-1018

Communication Briefings – Business & Management Skills
800-888-2086

SEMINAR INFORMATION FOR NETWORKERS

Seminar Corporation of America; 800-221-7464

CareerTrack Seminars & Tapes; 800-334-1018

American Management Association; 518-891-0065

SERVICE ORGANIZATIONS

Active 20-30 International
1915 I Street
Sacramento, CA 95814
916-447-3217

Active 20-30 US & Canada
1915 I Street
Sacramento, CA 95814
916-447-3217

Altrusa International, Inc.
332 S. Michigan Ave., Suite 1123
Chicago, IL 60604
312-427-4410

Canadian Jaycees
39 Leacock Way
Kanata, Ontario, Canada K2K 1T1
519-653-1920

Canadian Progress Club
2395 Bayview Avenue
North York, Ontario, Canada
M2L 1A2
416-446-1830

Civitan International
1401 52nd Street South
Birmingham, AL 35213
205-591-8910

Cosmopolitan International
7341 West 80th Street
Overland Park, KS 66204
913-648-4330

Jaycees
P.O. Box 140577
Coral Gables, FL 33114-0577
305-446-7608

Kiwanis International
3636 Woodview Trace
Indianapolis, IN 46268
317-875-8755

Lions Clubs International
300 22nd Street
Oak Brook, IL 60521-8842
708-571-5466

National Association of American
Business Clubs
3315 N. Main Street
High Point, NC 27262
929-869-2166

The National Exchange Club
3050 Central Avenue
Toledo, OH 43606
419-535-3232

National Federation of
Business and Professional Women
2012 Massachusetts Avenue, NW
Washington, DC 20036
202-293-1100

Optimist International
4494 Lindell Boulevard
St. Louis, MO 63108
314-371-6000

Pilot Club International
244 College Street
Macon, GA 31213-0599
912-743-7403

Quota International, Inc.
1420 21st Street, NW
Washington, DC 20036
202-331-9694

Rotary International
1560 Sherman Avenue
Evanston, IL 60201
708-866-3000

Round Table International
30707 Butia Palm
Homeland, CA 92348
714-926-4517

Ruritan National
P.O. Box 487, Ruritan Road
Dublin, VA 24084
703-674-5431

Sertoma International
1912 East Meyer Boulevard
Kansas City, MO 64132
816-333-8300

Soroptimist International
of the Americas
1616 Walnut Street, Suite 700
Philadelphia, PA 19103
215-732-0512

Toastmasters International
23182 Arroyo Vista
Rancha Santa Margarita, CA 92688
714-858-8255

Zonta International
557 W. Randolph Street
Chicago, IL 60606
312-930-5848

An Invitation from the Authors

Both Ken Erdman and Tom Sullivan present networking workshops and seminars of varying length. They also speak to corporations, trade associations, chambers of commerce, networking groups, civic clubs and service clubs.

For details or to arrange a seminar, workshop or speaking engagement, please contact:

The Three Marketeers, Inc.
402 Bethlehem Pike
Philadelphia, PA 19118
(215) 247-2787